Divine Echoes of Eternity

Daily Devotions on Hearing God

Noel Campbell
and
Linda Hanke

COPYRIGHT

Copyright © 2015, Noel Campbell and Linda Hanke
Published by Linda Hanke, hankelinda1@gmail.com

ALL RIGHTS RESERVED. This book contains material protected under International and Federal Copyright Laws and Treaties. Any unauthorized reprint or use of this material is prohibited. No part of this book may be reproduced or transmitted in any form or by any means, electronic or mechanical, including photocopying, recording, or by any information storage and retrieval system without express written permission from the author or publisher.

Cover Design by My Graphix Girl
Interior Design by Woven Red Author Services, WovenRed.ca

Divine Echoes of Eternity, Daily Devotions on Hearing God/Noel Campbell and Linda Hanke—1st edition

ISBN 978-0-692-39560-8

Unless otherwise indicated, all Scripture quotations are taken from the Holy Bible, New Living Translation, copyright © 1996, 2004, 2007 by Tyndale House Foundation. Used by permission of Tyndale House Publishers, Inc., Carol Stream, Illinois 60188. All rights reserved.

Copyright permission to retell the following stories has been granted by family members of Walter B. Knight, author of *Knight's Master Book of Illustrations*. WM EEDMANS PUBLISHING COMPANY, Grand Rapids, Michigan Copyright 1956: *Little Tug Boat, Acts of Love, An Answer in the Laundry, Pennies from Father, Forgiveness when it Counts, Secret of Contentment, The Cave and the Sun, Going to Heaven, Time with God, A Strong Foundation, The Building Code, Little Girl Teacher, From Heathens to Christians, Minnesota Miracle, I'm the Best Forgiveness when it Counts*.

Copyright permission was granted by David G. Benner to use the story *Time with God*, from his book *Opening to God*; Inter Varsity Press, Downer's Grove, IL, Copyright 2010.

Dedication

I, Noel, lovingly dedicate this book to my three sons and three daughters and their families.

I, Linda, would also like to dedicate this book to my precious children: my son Kevin and my daughter, Katrina and her family.

Acknowledgments

I am the discipleship pastor who taught for many years on the subjects in this book. I thank Linda Hanke for her years of faithfully attending my classes. She took my words, stories and concepts and put them in written form. A special thanks to Niki Anderson and Therese Marszalek for their wisdom and input. Much appreciation is extended to all my discipleship students, especially those whose stories are included in this daily devotional.

Endorsements

I have known Noel for nearly 40 years and always wondered when he would put his heart musings into a book. Now, Noel Campbell's *Divine Echoes of Eternity* puts an end to that wondering and brings a fresh beginning to a new journey with a man who is like Nathaniel, "Is one in whom there is no guile." You'll find yourself considering Noel a mentor by the time you're done reading this book, and if you're anything like me, you will be far richer because of it.

**—Wayne Cordeiro, Sr. Pastor and Founder
New Hope Christian Fellowship, Honolulu, Hawaii**

Divine Echoes of Eternity hits the bulls eye in answering questions that countless people have pondered about hearing God's voice. Multitudes of people around the globe have cried out to God to express their longing to know Him and communicate with Him. God heard those cries and is sending answers through anointed people like Pastor Noel Campbell and Linda Hanke, the team God called to birth *Divine Echoes of Eternity*. This power packed daily devotional demonstrates God's longing for His people to hear—and respond to—His voice as they live in constant communion with Him. What a blessing it was for me to see the excellent way in which Linda Hanke leads the reader through Pastor Noel's experiences as he learned how to listen to and follow the voice of the Good Shepherd throughout his life. For anyone desiring a closer walk with God, this devotional will launch you into each day with an impactful story based on scriptural truth, and will leave you with thought provoking questions to ponder throughout the day. I highly recommend this book as a regular staple for your spiritual diet. As you feast on and apply the truths shared in this God-inspired work, you'll find yourself even more hungry for a deeper intimacy with Him.

—Therese Marszalek, author of
40 Days of Devotional Journal and
From the Wilderness to the Miraculous
she is an Inspirational Speaker and has Therese Marszalek Ministries: Bringing Hope for Today

Noel Campbell is the wisest man I know.

I first met Noel when I was 15. The man who introduced us had told me that Noel was a man's man who exhibited gentleness, a fruit of the Spirit, to a rare degree. He misspoke. Noel exhibited *all* the fruit of the Spirit to a rare degree, and especially love.

When I began to work with Noel in youth ministry, the first thing he taught me was that we were to love students. I learned how to do that by watching him.

I've been watching him now for more than 45 years. Noel has been my friend, mentor, pastor, and example. Did I mention that he is also my father-in-law? Some accused me of marrying Laina so I could get Noel as a father!

Noel is a Jesus-man through and through. He listens to Jesus and follows. At our church, he teaches discipleship classes—at 85, he is still passionate about following Jesus and helping others follow Him.

When Noel speaks, I listen. I hope you will too.

—Joe Wittwer Head Pastor of Life Center Church
Spokane, Washington

Introduction

Noel and I collaborated to write this book. Why did I help write it? Let me tell you a little about myself and you'll understand. When I was five, my mother died of a brain tumor and two years later, my father succumbed to his alcoholism leaving me an orphan. My siblings and I spent many years in foster homes (not sure how many) until my oldest sister rescued us from the last abusive home. I grew up as best I could. In my 30's, and after many struggles, I came to faith in Christ. Years later sitting in a church, I heard Noel Campbell preach on love. This pastor spoke gently but passionately about loving people unconditionally. I sat in the pew thinking, *Could love really be like that? Is this man for real?*

Indeed, both love and Noel are for real. Over the years, I've watched him win the hearts of hundreds of people and for thirteen years I have gleaned wisdom from him while I sat in his discipleship classes. Noel has gleaned great wisdom from the Lord that he and I believe needs to be shared far beyond the discipleship classes.

As you read the devotions, you will gain a greater understanding of the Lord's radical love for you and how to extend that kind of love to others with a newfound kindness and mercy. You will grasp the importance of true forgiveness and sacrificial living from stories shared about his student's adventures.

God is always waiting to guide our paths and He

does so as we listen to Him and obey His directions. Unique tales of His guidance will bring laughter, joy and a sense of awe. Here is his book—daily devotions from his life, stories from his students, and examples that reveal Biblical truths. This man of God has richly mentored me. May you also be mentored by Noel as you daily discover the wisdom he received from God.

—Linda Hanke

Table of Contents

Father's Loving Gaze 1
Up in Flames 3
Pure Clean Water 5
"As Is" Love 7
Sacrifice Your Wings 9
Take a Risk 11
What's for Dinner? 13
The Christmas Present 15
Love Makes the Difference 17
Look Up, Soar High 19
The Thrill of Flying 21
Enjoying Fruit 23
We Made It! 25
Tattoo Tony Lives On 27
He Opens Prison Doors 29
Janitor with a Heart 31
For Better or Worse 33
Mistreating God—Not a Good Idea 35
Ice Cream for Dinner! 37
Hot Dog Prayers 39
Love the Game! 41
Trusting Mom and Dad 43
Burned at the Stake 45

Prayer Saved the Day 47
Change of Plans.. 49
Get Out of the Way!... 51
A Close Call... 53
Just in Time 55
Unconscious in the Road 57
A Difficult Departure.. 59
Cry Out to God... 61
What Do I Wear?... 63
Animals on Board 65
Loved and Cherished 67
Lost It All 69
Go Home!.. 71
Carry the Load 73
He's Saved!.. 75
Niagara Falls Excursion 77
Spotting a Bear 79
Go Back to Sleep 81
Bad Timing... 83
The Entrance Requirement 85
Help!... 87
Generosity of a King.. 89
Don't Trust Snakes!... 91
Two Men—Two Options... 93
A Son is Saved 95
It's Not Worth It! 97

Confused Priorities	99
Got the Job!	101
It's Too Crowded	103
Mother-in-law Jokes	105
See You in Heaven	107
God Provides	109
From Atheist to Christian	111
Perfect Guidance	113
Lost and Scared	115
Locked Out and No Key	117
Prison Converts	119
Offer Up Your Praises	121
Angels Visited	123
Record Breaking Days	125
God Runs the Company	127
Bad Decision!	129
Ministry in Africa	131
Live Prudently	133
The Manufacturer's Design	135
Speaking Love Words	137
Surprised by Change	139
Kindness Won Out	141
Beauty Salon Caper	143
The Holy Spirit Moved	145
Lucy Looking Out	147
Storm is Coming	149

Gypsy Ran	151
Prayer for Marriage	153
Act of Service	155
Learning from Fire	157
An Amazing Man	159
Trust, Rely On and Cling	161
Unfairly Represented	163
Denounce Jesus!	165
A Godly Man	167
A Child's Faith	169
A Loving Grandmother	171
A Prayer for a Neighbor	173
Landing My Plane	175
No More Glacier Park	177
At the Top	179
Rescued from a Ditch	181
Contact Lens Caper	183
First Prize Winner	185
First Time Ever Said	187
Passing the Test	189
Throw Them Away!	191
Singing for Jesus	193
Two for One Special	195
Train Up a Child	197
Bowling Ball in a China Closet	199
Going in Circles	201

Holding Dad's Hand	203
Monday's a Comin'!	205
One Huge Dog	207
Out in the Cold	208
Bible by My Side	210
She Stopped Singing	212
Shave Your Beard!	214
I'm Lost!	216
A Confused Skunk	218
Don't Go Hunting	220
A New Direction	222
Look, Grandma!	224
Life Threatening Adventure	226
Hissing Snakes	228
Don't Be Concerned	230
Stop Praying for Him	232
The Lost Finger	234
Spit in the Face	236
Here I Come, God	238
Green Apples	240
Parenting God's Way	242
Mafia Man	244
My Mother's Face	246
A Book that Saved Me	248
Treasure of Life	250
Three More Years	252

Love Your Brothers 254
We are Receivers 256
The Little Tugboat 258
I'm the Best! 260
Acts of Love 262
An Answer in the Laundry 264
Pennies from Father 266
Time with God 268
A Strong Foundation 270
The Building Code 272
Forgiveness When It Counts 274
Going to Heaven 276
Little Girl Teacher 278
Why Aren't You Here? 280
From Heathens to Christians 282
Secret of Contentment 284
The Cave and the Sun 286
Minnesota Miracle 288

Father's Loving Gaze

This is real love—not that we loved God but that He loved us and sent His Son as a sacrifice to take away our sins. (John 1:4—10)

At 38, I became a widower when my wife died of cancer. I suffered a great loss at her passing, but God's presence comforted me. Knowing I had the task of raising six precious children alone, I moved forward for their sake. Wonderful memories remain of my wife and of the children when they were young. Over the years, coming home from work and cuddling each child brought me immeasurable contentment. Love filled my heart as I looked into their sweet faces and listened to their chatter.

I adored those babes, but they were unaware of their emotional and financial expense to me. My exhaustion did not disturb their sleep. My pain did not stop their play. My empty wallet they couldn't fill. Nevertheless, love flowed freely and extravagantly from me to each of them.

I am convinced, that is the way God loves. John the disciple tells us that God loved us so much that He sent His son to die for our sins. Genuine love flows from the

Lord, and He needs nothing to activate it because He *is* love. He guides, instructs, protects, comforts, talks and listens to us.

His divine love is selfless with no conditions attached. Jesus, His own Son, died so we could be in heaven for all eternity. What greater expense could there have been? Yet, each person is deeply cherished in this extravagant way by the God of the universe.

Thoughts to Ponder

Have you ever stopped to contemplate the deep love God has for you? This is the kind of love that would sacrifice His own son on your behalf. You don't have to do anything, but just receive it—like a little child in his parent's arms. Take time to picture the Lord gazing at you with adoring eyes and be confident of His sheer delight in you.

Up in Flames

Human anger does not produce the righteousness God desires. *(James 1:20)*

The headlines in a 1937 newspaper read, "When Flames Engulfed World's Greatest Airship." The Germans introduced their new invention, the Hindenburg Zeppelin, which they hailed as the solution to transporting passengers across the ocean. According to one theory, all went well until a mechanic hammered a nail on the wooden base of this large balloon, which caused a spark that set the Zeppelin ablaze. When it exploded, this once great experiment in flying was completely destroyed. The demise of the Hindenburg came from the use of helium gas and a spark that ignited it.

Likewise, the demise of a relationship can come from the wrong kind of emotional fuel. Love can often be conditional. When things don't go the way we prefer, we can explode in anger. The Bible says, "Anger does not produce the righteousness God desires." We may think everything is going well in our interaction with others, until we experience a clash of ideas or hurt feelings. Like the Hindenburg, all can come crashing down if our relationships are not based on pure, unconditional love. This kind of love is filled with grace, acceptance and a willingness to listen, learn and forgive. Giving those you love another chance when they make a mistake, listening carefully to their point of view and releasing hurt feelings go a long way in sustaining a healthy relationship.

Thoughts to Ponder

What kind of relational fuel are you using? Are you quick to blow up in anger leaving others feeling emotionally destroyed? Try unconditional love and extending grace. You will have a greater chance of safely soaring high.

Pure Clean Water

> The purpose of my instruction is that all believers would be filled with love that comes from a pure heart, a clean conscience and a sincere faith.
> *(Timothy 1:1—5)*

"Drinking dirty water? Yuck!" my friend said as we talked one morning.

After he asked me if I wanted a drink, I suggested a glass of water. We sat and discussed his difficulty with relationships while consuming it. I gave little thought to the glass and its contents, until I looked and realized it had everything to do with our conversation.

"Now just suppose when you handed me this water, it was murky and dirty instead of pure and clean. Do you think I would have wanted to drink it?" I questioned.

My friend was alarmed and absolutely opposed the idea. Well, that's the same thing when relating to others," I gently chided him. In the Bible, Timothy wrote that God instructed us to have love that is pure, sincere and from a good conscience.

The pattern of the world can often be murky and dirty; God's way is always clean and pure. The world's way of living is selfish ambition. God's way is self-sacrifice. The world's way is strife and trying to get ahead of others. God's way is putting others' needs above our own. The world's way is a question of who is right and wrong. God's way brings peace and reconciliation.

Thoughts to Ponder

What kind of water are you serving to others? More importantly, *how are you interacting with them?* Be sure your actions come from a pure heart, a clean conscience and a sincere faith.

"As Is" Love

For God loved the world so much that He gave his one and only Son so that everyone who believes in Him will not perish but have eternal life. (John 3:16)

"What? I can really be loved the way I am?" Over the years I have heard this question expressed in many ways. It is my desire that people understand God's amazing love for them just the way He created them. Recently, I listened to my son-in-law preach on "as is" love. He is the pastor of a large church in the Pacific Northwest and is known for his candor and frankness.

Many times I have watched the congregation respond to his vulnerability in sharing his weaknesses and faults. Speaking from the pulpit what few pastors would admit about themselves, he gains him followers who can more readily grow in their faith. For example, he shares about angrily yelling at his children when they were little, and thinking negative thoughts about someone who has criticized him until the Lord reminds him of the need to forgive.

God loves us so much, even when we are not perfect, that he gave His Son to die for us. As Christians, we probably know John 3:16, but do we understand what it really means? "As is" love is a characteristic of God. He loves us "as is" with impure thoughts and actions, "as is" with bitterness and anger affecting those around us, "as is" with addictions and habits causing harm to ourselves and others. Yes, God loves us with every fault and failure.

Thoughts to Ponder

Do you understand this simple but complex truth? Knowing God's "as is" love brings freedom. Always remember you are loved by the God of the universe. Come to Him just as you are and allow Him to bring you into all He designed you to be.

Sacrifice Your Wings

Live a life filled with love following the example of Christ. He loved us and offered Himself as a sacrifice for us, a pleasing aroma to God. *(Ephesians 5:2)*

My mother, whom I loved dearly, was a remarkable woman. I was an only child, and she put me and my father's needs far above her own. Mom, however, was a fanatic about safety, and both Dad and I felt the restriction.

Mom's daunting desire to stop Dad from flying planes, a hobby he thoroughly wanted to pursue, won out. Even though flying planes in the 1930's was risky, the idea intrigued him, but Dad loved Mom so much that he sacrificed his dreams. Over the years, I wondered if he was right to abandon his dream.

The answer to my question is found in Christ. "He loved us and offered himself as a sacrifice for us, a pleasing aroma to God." Sacrificing our wishes for another is the character of God. We are most like Him when we let go of what we want out of deference for the one we love. My mother's fears may have been somewhat extreme, but my father's love was sacrificial.

Thoughts to Ponder

How often do you stop and consider not what's best for you, but what's best for the one you love? Yes, this can be done, but what about those times when the cost seems high? When the request from the one you love seems unreasonable? That is the time to consider Christ's amazing sacrifice for you.

Take a Risk

Don't forget to show hospitality to strangers, for some who have done this have entertained angels without realizing it! *(Hebrews 13:2)*

Home alone and in a rough part of town, my daughter let a dubious looking man into her house. He was a book salesman who appeared like he needed to make a sale. After saying a quick prayer and confident that she heard God's voice, Liane invited the man in and listened to his sales pitch. It was a good one, and within a short time she purchased $60 worth of books, and gave him an extra $20.

Little did he know, however, what else he would receive when he knocked on her door; Liane had a sales pitch, as well. The man cautiously listened, considered it and bought her product—Jesus. When he left her house, he was a changed man.

I would never recommend inviting a strange man in except for the certainty of hearing from the Lord. I do know, however, my daughter put God's love in action. As far as Liane knew, this man was not an angel, but someone in need of the Lord. She had money to buy his product, extra money to give him, and to tell him what he needed most—the love of Jesus.

Thoughts to Ponder

Have you ever entertained strangers with kindness and loving hospitality—even when it might be a little risky? I am not suggesting putting yourself in danger; however, at the Lord's leading, you can make an eternal difference in someone's life. Why not practice being alert to such opportunities?

What's for Dinner?

> Since God chose you to be the holy people He loves, you must clothe yourselves with tenderhearted mercy, kindness, humility, gentleness and patience. *(Colossians 3:12)*

Single-parenting six children had its challenges, and I am so glad God was by my side through it all. Over the years, as my three daughters became teenagers, they each asked if they could prepare dinner. I agreed, and it became a great learning experience for them.

One night, my youngest daughter, Liane, set dinner on the table, which brought a resounding round of complaints from one of my young sons. Tears filled her eyes as she went back into the kitchen. I was about to reprimand my son when I heard a loud noise: the electric mixer. Moments later, Liane returned and set a large chocolate milkshake in front of him. Needless to say, he was pleased!

As a small boy, my son had not yet mastered the art of graciousness. My daughter however, learned her lessons from Jesus' teachings. Mercy, kindness, gentleness and patience characterized her behavior, and I can only think Jesus smiled as she set the chocolate milkshake in front of her brother. To this day, that son and daughter live close to each other, and they and their families are best of friends.

Thoughts to Ponder

How do you act when you are offended? Do you lash back, retreat and walk away or do you think about blessing the other person? A gesture of kindness and love will bring pleasure to God as you respond with tender-hearted mercy. You may also be surprised how much better you feel.

The Christmas Present

> If I had the gift of prophecy, and I understood all of God's secret plans and possessed all knowledge, and if I had such faith that I could move mountains, but didn't love others, I would be nothing.
> (1 Corinthians 3:2)

One Christmas, I gave my daughter, Liane, a silk scarf I thought she would enjoy, and I often looked to see if she wore it, but she never did. Receiving gifts is fun, but giving gifts brings me greater pleasure even though I never quite know what to buy. I didn't fret over the fact that I never saw her wear it; my gift was only a scarf, and it was of little significance in the grand scheme of things. However, this experience often made me wonder if there are gifts God has given us that we are not using.

Loving others is utmost to our Creator because love is His identifying quality and nothing is more central to His character. My daughter never wore the scarf I gave her, but one thing I know about her is the gift she has to love others. An extremely caring and nurturing mother, she is quick to think of others before herself. The central quality in my parenting was teaching my children the importance of loving others. Liane didn't wear the scarf, but she wears love, and it is beautiful on her. I thank God that she received and is using that gift.

Thoughts to Ponder

Are there gifts you have received and are not using? The gifts given others are nice to use, but the real treasures God gives are the ones you want to put into practice. Especially the gift of love, it is a gift that will bless God, you and those who receive it.

Love Makes the Difference

Dear friends, let us continue to love one another, for love comes from God. Anyone who loves is a child of God and knows God. (1 John 4:7)

I stood out like a sore thumb. Everything about me was different. When I became a logger in the woods of Western Oregon, I lived in a logging camp alongside rough, tough men with language that mirrored their lifestyle. It was a daily challenge to work with them, but my faith in God sustained me. I remained steadfast in what I believed and exhibited kindness and love at every opportunity.

Long after I had left logging to become a pharmacist, my old boss searched for me until he found me. His son had died, and I was the only "man of God" he knew. He asked me to officiate at his son's funeral, and I became reacquainted with him in his time of crisis. He listened carefully as I told him of my love for Jesus, and he asked Jesus into his heart. After he died, his family again found me to officiate at his funeral. The Bible says that we as Christians "will be known by our love." That logging boss saw God's love in me, and it caused him to find me in his time of need.

Thoughts to Ponder

Are you known by your love? People are watching even when you don't realize it. Those who know you are a Christian may be watching you even closer because they have expectations of you. Don't disappoint them, show the love of Christ. You may make a great difference in their lives and point them to Christ.

Look Up, Soar High

> For I can do everything through Christ, who gives me strength. *(Philippians 4:13)*

Have you ever settled for second best? You may think you can't accomplish your dream and have even been told by others that it's impossible. Ted W. Engstrom tells a story in his book, *The Pursuit of Excellence,* about a prairie chicken that was an eagle, but didn't know it.

As he tells the story, a mother prairie chicken was about to raise a family. She got the nest ready, laid her eggs and went out looking for food. While she was gone, someone placed an eagle egg in her nest with the others. In time they all hatched, and the mother prairie chicken along with her brood went walking along on the ground, scratching for bugs and worms. The little eagle got bigger and bigger, but still assumed she was a prairie chicken.

One day, she looked up and saw a bird soaring high in the sky. "Wouldn't it be fun to fly high up in the air?" she asked her siblings.

"You can't fly; you're a chicken!" they all laughed.

So she sighed and said, "You must be right." She spent the rest of her life scratching on the ground, looking for bugs and worms.

That eagle let others define her. She missed the thrill of soaring in the clouds and experiencing freedom. You don't have to miss the great promise from God. He loves you so much He wants you to succeed in all He has for you. Don't give up when others say you can't accomplish what you know God wants you to do. His love will strengthen your resolve to make it to the destination He planned for you from the beginning of time.

Thoughts to Ponder

Are you soaring high or looking down? If you depend on God's love for you, you will be in the just right place. Don't give up when others say you can't. Look up and realize you can do all things through Christ.

The Thrill of Flying

> But I say, love your enemies. Pray for those who persecute you! *(Matthew 5:44)*

Soaring high above the clouds and gliding low over the fields brought me blissful sensations of peace and freedom. I wasn't an observer; I was a full-fledged participant. Occasionally, I have watched an air show, but it is nothing like the thrill of flying a plane, swooping through the air doing acrobatic stunts. In comparison, watching planes perform from the ground seemed like a waste of time.

I have found a similar experience in other areas of my life. Loving someone who has harmed me has sometimes been beyond what I thought I could do. I have remembered, however, that Jesus' love has no limits. In fact, He loved us so much that while on the cross He asked God to forgive the people who put Him there.

Jesus said, "Love your enemies! Pray for those who persecute you." There have been times when I would have much rather been soaring high in my plane than extending this kind of love! But when I did, I found a great amount of freedom and peace of mind.

Thoughts to Ponder

Think about your enemies. Can you ponder ways to show acts of love to them? Obeying God by loving your enemies is God's way that leads you to a new plateau in your walk with the Lord.

Enjoying Fruit

> But the Holy Spirit produces this kind of fruit in our lives: love, joy, peace, patience, kindness, goodness, faithfulness, gentleness and self-control.
> (*Galatians* 5:22)

"Not everything is easily digested," explained Kim, a discipleship student of mine. When teaching on the fruit of the Spirit, I asked the participants of my class to write the names of each fruit on a separate piece of paper, put them in a container, and draw out one every morning for a week, and then put that fruit into practice for the day. "Have fun," I encouraged them as they left the class that Sunday morning.

The following week, Kim shared her experience. For months, family members had told her she needed more patience. The first morning of her assignment, she was certain she would draw patience and was looking forward to working on her perceived shortcoming. To her surprise, she drew love, so she went about her day practicing loving those around her.

The second day, she again drew love. Kim continued to find ways of being loving but looked forward to practicing patience. However, to her chagrin, the third day, love was drawn again. In fact, every day for the entire week she drew the same fruit of the Spirit.

By the end of the week, she was perplexed and inquired of the Lord, "What is going on? I know I need patience, why didn't I draw it?" Kim proceeded to inform God she learned unlimited ways of showing love but really needed to work on her patience. *Don't you get it, if you just love people the way I want you to, you will be patient.* Those words the Lord spoke to Kim at that moment came as a pleasant surprise.

Kim had "eaten all the fruit" she needed. Her relationships were enhanced, and she successfully completed the assignment.

Thoughts to Ponder

Want to grow lots of fruit? Then produce the virtuous fruits of the Spirit. You will experience your relationships growing sweeter and sweeter! You can practice this same thing by putting slips of paper with the fruits of the Spirit listed on them and put them into a vase. Draw one out each morning and exercise it in your daily life. Remember the fruits of the Spirit are love, joy, peace, patience, kindness, goodness, faithfulness, gentleness and self-control.

We Made It!

> Love is patient, love is kind. Love is not jealous or boastful or proud. It does not demand its own way. It is not irritable and keeps no record of being wronged.
> *(1 Corinthians 13:4)*

"Our marriage was coming unraveled." Sue confided in me many years after the fact. She and her husband Steve, my fellow co-worker, struggled with their communication, and Steve consulted me often about his and Sue's relationship. Sue explained that her husband exhorted her frequently with suggestions I had given him on how to make their communication better. Before long, she became tired of hearing more advice until the day Steve announced that he had invited me to their home to counsel them.

"I thought I finally had the chance to share my side," Sue declared. "However, in your caring but matter-of-fact way, you sat down, opened your Bible and began sharing scripture without giving me a chance to explain about Steve."

"Love is patient, love is kind" and on you went quoting from 1 Corinthians 13, the love chapter of the Bible. You advised us to love each other unconditionally, you prayed and left. Afterwards, I cried in frustration, yet I had a strong feeling you were sharing just what we needed to hear." Laughing, Sue concluded, "Somehow, the love chapter took root in our hearts and within months, our marriage greatly improved."

Surprised to hear Sue's side of the story long after I had counseled with them, I shot up a prayer of thanksgiving to God. I often marvel at the truth of God's word. Not demanding your own way, not being irritable, and keeping no record of wrongs can turn an unhappy relationship into one of joy.

Thoughts to Ponder

Take time to consider your relationship. Could the love chapter make a difference? Allow yourself time to slowly read and contemplate what the scriptures say in 1 Corinthians 13:4 through 8. You may be surprised about the difference it makes in your interactions with your marriage partner.

Tattoo Tony Lives On

Jesus looked at them intently and said, "Humanly speaking it is impossible. But with God everything is possible." *(Matthew 19:26)*

"A miracle in the making, something I would have never believed fifteen years ago."

Ron, my discipleship student, tells of his encounter with a rough, stocky, body-building inmate covered with piercings and known as Tattoo Tony. Ron first met him while visiting kids in the local detention center.

When Tony was 16, he was a likeable kid eager to hear about Jesus and read the Bible. However, this became his first of many lock-up experiences with several more stays at the detention center, city hall, county jail, and then prison for committing armed robbery. Addiction to drugs and alcohol became an almost insurmountable challenge. Ron visited Tony during each of his incarcerations. "Giving up on Tony was never an option. I just kept reminding him of Jesus' love and stayed in contact with him wherever he ended up," recalls Ron.

Now at 31, Tony has been out of prison and free from drugs for eight years. He has a good job, a beautiful wife and leads Bible studies at his church. Sound impossible? Nothing is impossible with God. God's love has no limits, and through Ron's perseverance, Tony made it. Drug-free with a changed life, Tony is now considered a miracle. Ron's love and tenacity became the instruments God used to accomplish His purposes. The impossible is possible with the Lord.

Thoughts to Ponder

Can you *really* believe that when all seems hopeless, God can do anything? If God can change a hardened criminal into a Bible study teacher, He can intervene in your circumstances and make a radical difference.

He Opens Prison Doors

Oh, how great are God's riches and wisdom and knowledge! How impossible it is for us to understand His decisions and His ways. (Romans 11:33)

"I threw away all my medications. Now it was time to experience the love and faithfulness of God." Robin had attended my classes for a year before sharing her story. She had struggled with fear and sickness, and therefore never left her home. She found it difficult to breathe when away from the security of her self-imposed prison.

Knowing she was slowly headed for destruction, Robin began reading her Bible and calling out to God. She started to understand God's love for her, and as she prayed, her trust in God grew. For years she had been plagued with asthma, food allergies, anxiety and unaligned bones. One day she felt she heard God tell her to go off her medications, and He would heal her. Robin decided to trust God and stopped taking her pills. Within weeks, she was healed. She began coming to church and found her way to my discipleship classes.

When Robin came to the end of herself, she called out to God and discovered the love and great riches of God. Transformed by her trust in the Lord, the door of

Robin's self-imposed prison swung open to a new life of self-confidence and freedom.

Although I do not recommend going completely off medications without sound medical advice or clear instruction from the Lord, I do recommend turning to God in total trust, believing His love can intervene in any circumstance.

Thoughts to Ponder

Do you have a self-imposed prison keeping you from freedom? Fear? Anger? Unforgiveness? Call out to God. He can swing the door open. Stop trying to take care of your problems alone. Give them to God; His ways are filled with wisdom and knowledge.

Janitor with a Heart

If you love me, obey My commandments. (John 14:15)

From social worker to janitor—now that's quite a career change! My friend Linda worked with teen moms living on public assistance. Long hours and stress had led to burnout, so she quit her job. Since employment was still a necessity for her, she pursued other job opportunities.

Hearing of a janitor position at the church, Linda quickly dismissed the idea thinking, *I've got a master's degree in social work, why would I want to be a janitor?* Then one day while praying, she felt strongly that the Lord wanted her to take the job. *Can this be the Lord?* She wondered. Later that afternoon at a Christian bookstore, Linda came across a poster with a clear message.

The poster displayed a picture of a church with stained glass windows. Kneeling at the altar two people were praying, and in the forefront stood a woman with a mop in her hand. The caption at the bottom said, "It is not the bended knee that counts, it's the bended heart." Linda knew this was a word for her from the Lord and quickly took the position at the church.

Five years later, Linda was back in social work knowing her years as a janitor increased her insight of God's ways. Although degrees and education can be important, God cares about humility, sacrifice and service to others. Her love of God and desire to obey him led to her growth as a person and social worker. Obeying God has great rewards—even when His requests seem difficult.

Thoughts to Ponder

Are you willing to follow God's guidance even when His request seems difficult? We have a choice to say yes or no to God when He leads us on life's journey. It's easier to say yes to those things that make sense or aren't difficult, but what about those requests that are hard to obey? Resolve to follow God's leading anyway; you will be surprised at what you learn.

For Better or Worse

We know what real love is because Jesus gave up His life for us. So we also ought to give up our lives for our brothers and sisters. *(1 John 3:16)*

"Gary has been my true love throughout our marriage and has always been there for me when I needed him," Colleen, a discipleship student, said. "For better or worse, I will always be there for him as well." Gary's progressive dementia put their marriage on a new journey. As she shared stories of their life together, her classmates acquired a deeper understanding of selfless love.

One of the signs of dementia came when Gary put his shoes on the opposite feet and wore them half a day before Colleen noticed. Another day Gary put his wallet in his sock and walked out the door ready to go somewhere, but he didn't know his destination or that his wallet belonged in his pocket.

"Life is a challenge," she admits to the class. "But I wouldn't have it any other way." Gary was once an easygoing man with a contagious smile; he was someone everybody respected. "But to this day," Colleen says, "the last words he speaks at bedtime are, 'I love you,

Honey.'" Colleen indicates those are special words to her because he now speaks infrequently. Also, because he loses his balance, she has no idea how much longer she can care for him. This is unconditional love, and Colleen has *given her life* to be there for her husband.

Thoughts to Ponder

When have you needed to show this kind of love and go the extra mile with your spouse? That extra mile may seem to go a long way or require much from you. That mile may go on a lifetime. Yes, for better or worse there may be unexpected implications; but as you press on, you may find unexpected rewards.

Mistreating God—Not a Good Idea

> This is real love—not that we loved God, but that He loved us and sent His Son as a sacrifice to take away our sins. *(1 John 4:10)*

A man kicked the dog once—then kicked him again. The dog yelped in pain and then hobbled slowly over to the man and licked his hand. I heard about this incident and thought, *Yes, a dog is man's best friend, even when it is being mistreated.*

Not intending to link the dog with God, or me with that angry man, nevertheless, I see some similarities. I sometimes ask myself, *what kind of Christian am I?* I had Godly parents, was raised in the church and, as long as I can remember, I have loved Jesus. I walk with Him, talk with Him and have dedicated my life to serving Him. However, with an uneasy feeling, I wonder how often I mistreat him.

I ponder, *what do I do for God? What do I give Him?* I can hurt Him, neglect Him, and ignore Him. I can do my own thing and make my own plans. If I get lost, He comes looking for me and He still loves me. The Lord saved me, took away my sins and gave me eternal life. This is real love, and I am thankful for it.

Thoughts to Ponder

How are you treating the God of the Universe? Do you ever mistreat Him? Forget to thank Him or praise Him? Ignore His voice? He is always ready to love you.

Ice Cream for Dinner!

Love each other with genuine affection, and take delight in honoring each other. (Romans 12:10)

Ice cream for supper—"Yeah, I love it!" the kids shouted. On occasion, my daughter, Laina, and her husband had ice cream for the main course of their meal. All five of their children loved those dinners. Laina usually cooked nutritional meals, but an ice cream meal delighted the children now and then. My grandkids would excitedly blurt out their favorite flavors: "Vanilla! Chocolate! Strawberry!" Each child was anticipating the cold, creamy substance sliding over their tongue as they consumed a hardy bowl of it. If it had tasted bad, there would have been a resounding "Yuck!" at the mention of it.

But saying, "I love ice cream," is much different than saying, for instance, "I love my wife." Ice cream is only loved for what it can do for you. That is conditional. Hopefully, saying, "I love my wife," comes with no conditions attached. I love her "for better or worse." Unconditional love says I will love you no matter what. We are to love others "with genuine affection" given to us by God.

Thoughts to Ponder

Do you love in spite of complaining, messiness, or lack of understanding? Do you still love when he leaves the seat up? Comes home late for dinner? Adds an extra twenty pounds? Do you love others or your spouse with a commitment far more than the love of ice cream, no matter what flavor they bring to the table?

Hot Dog Prayers

So encourage each other and build each other up, just as you are already doing. (1 Thessalonians 5:11)

Bruce, a member of my class, traveled to California with his wife, Val, to visit her parents. While visiting, they left her parents' house to go to the park and read.

The temperature soared into the nineties, so they found a covered bench near a hot dog vendor. They sat down and settled in; however, their attention was drawn to the vendor, watching him talk to many people who were buying his food. Bruce listened and instantly felt the man's voice reminded him of Jesus.

Curious, Bruce and Val approached the stand and found him praying for his customers. As they talked, Bruce learned the man loved the Lord and looked for opportunities to talk about God with everyone who bought a hot dog. This man wept when Bruce told him his voice sounded like Jesus' voice. "That's the nicest thing anyone ever said to me," he declared.

Bruce knew the value of "building each other up in their faith," and he made a difference in the hot dog salesman's life that day.

Thoughts to Ponder

Have you encouraged anyone in the faith lately? Let the love of God spur you on to offer a good word to a fellow Christian who is faithfully serving the Lord. You never know the encouragement you can bring to a fellow believer.

Love the Game!

> Love each other with genuine, affection, and delight in honoring each other. *(Romans 12:10)*

The ball came whizzing by me, and I smashed it with all my might. Racquetball—I love that sport! I played it for 30 years. I taught my son Greg to play, and he won several state awards.

It's exhilarating, a great work-out, and challenging. For many years there was not a sport I liked doing more. Staying focused is mandatory; quick bursts of energy are required, and steady follow-through wins the game. I loved playing. It would not have been nearly as much fun if I had sat and watched.

So it is with unconditional love. It's not a spectator sport. The excitement comes with joining in; I played racquetball with all my might. In the same way, loving wholeheartedly takes going forward into a relationship with all you have. God's Word says, "Love each other with genuine affection." It's not just instructing us to love others; it's asking us to genuinely show love for them. Entering in, staying connected and not giving up wins the day.

Thoughts to Ponder

Do you back off when a friend is in trouble, or do you persevere and pray until he is through the crisis? Real love sticks. What do you think? *Pure love takes action.* Don't sit by and watch—get in the game!

Trusting Mom and Dad

> But Jesus overheard them and said to Jairus, "Don't be afraid, just have faith." *(Mark 5:36)*

There were bills to pay, a child to feed, a meager income and no foreseeable change in circumstances. Living during the great depression brought many challenges, but did those challenges concern me? Not at all! As a little boy living through those turbulent years, I didn't have a clue what we were experiencing.

My faith hinged on the loving care of my parents. I trusted them and played happily by their side believing all was well with me. That is what Jesus wants from us—simple faith that knows all is well no matter what. God, our parent, vigilantly cares for all of his children.

God's word says to be free of fear. As a child, I focused on my father and mother, content that they would provide for me. Hardships must have surrounded our home, and my parents must have faced difficulties daily. Yet as a young child, I didn't look at those circumstances; I knew to look only to my mother and father.

Thoughts to Ponder

What do you do during times of difficulty? Can you focus on your Heavenly Father? In doing so, you can find rest and peace. Jesus offers perfect advise, "Don't be afraid, and just have faith."

Burned at the Stake

> Each of us has been assigned a measure of faith.
> (Romans 12:3)

One by one, they died for their faith. Not willing to deny their belief in God, each one succumbed to being tied to a stake and set on fire. *Foxes Book of Martyrs* lists the names and dates of these men and women who suffered for Christ.

I love to read, but reading these accounts gave me butterflies in my stomach as I pondered the fate of these courageous saints.

"How could I ever do that?" I asked the Lord.

His response settled my heart. *If I asked you to do it, I would give you what you needed to obey.*

How reassuring! No matter what we face in life, God provides the measure of faith we need. Few of us will die a martyr's death, but most of us will face heartache and pain. I can look back on several difficult periods; the death of my wife, raising six children alone, job loss and financial loss. Yes, those were difficult days, but God provided me the faith I needed to trust Him.

Thoughts to Ponder

Are you enduring a hardship right now? Does it seem to be more than you can handle? Be reassured, you will be given the faith you require if you trust in the Lord for it.

Prayer Saved the Day

> Faith is the confidence that what we hope for will actually happen. *(Hebrews 11:1)*

Looking toward the shore, the ship's crew saw people preparing a fire. The crew trembled realizing they were to be these natives' evening meal. Hudson Taylor, a man known for his great faith, was among the men on this ship as he traveled to China. The book, *Hudson Taylor's Spiritual Secret,* shares this event, saying that while they were traveling to their destination, the winds ceased. Hudson's ship sat helplessly in the ocean, slowly drifting to shore where the natives were waiting.

Mr. Taylor confidently told the captain that all was not lost because the Christians on board would pray. He suggested to the unbelieving second officer to let down the mainsail because a breeze was coming. Immediately, the winds came and the ship continued on its way.

Hudson possessed a vital quality when he prayed: total assurance that his prayers would be answered. He became known for receiving whatever he asked or prayed. His dependence on the Lord brought ongoing results that few others have experienced. A hundred and fifty years later, Hudson Taylor is still regarded as an amazing man of prayer.

Praying with faith is the key ingredient for successful prayers. Effective prayer is not a matter of length, the words used, or how loudly you pray. It is a matter of knowing resolutely that when you call out to God, He hears and will answer.

Thoughts to Ponder

Are you confident when you pray? Try talking to God with deep, abiding trust, pray His will, and watch confidently for the answer. Others will grow in their faith as they observe your faith in action.

Change of Plans

My thoughts are nothing like your thoughts says the Lord, and my ways are far beyond anything you could imagine. *(Isaiah 55:8)*

Looking up at the clock, I sighed. *Only 7:00 p.m. and still three more hours to go.* Here I was, stocking shelves at a local grocery store, while working part-time as a dorm assistant and attending the school of pharmacy full time. This had not been the plan I had for my life, however, God had made it clear to me that it was His plan.

I had been playing football at Oregon State College and majoring in forestry. A scholarship provided financial stability while I attended school. Then I heard the Lord's still small voice encouraging the transition from forestry to pharmacy. This meant giving up football and my lucrative financial provision to work two jobs while I completed a rigorous program at pharmacy school.

God had a good reason when He led me in a different direction. I did not understand the reason. However, His thoughts are higher than mine, and I am glad I chose to follow Him.

Although I encountered difficult days, I never regretted making the change. Following God's plan brought me to the place of meeting my wife and a fulfilling 30-year career as a pharmacist. I did not understand why, but I knew that when God led in a different direction for my life, He had a good reason.

Thoughts to Ponder

Do you believe God has plans for your life? Don't follow your own ideas by leaning on your own understanding. God's ways are always best because He knows what the future holds. Make it your goal to listen to His direction and follow Him if he changes your course. You can be confident His guidance will be perfect.

Get Out of the Way!

For if we obey Him, everything will turn out well for us. (Jeremiah 42:66)

Move! The Lord's voice boomed in my head. Instantly, I jumped to the side. Before I hit the ground, a thick, heavy cable began piling up where I had been standing. If I had not listened to the Lord, a ton of steel would have crushed me.

In my logging days, I worked on a coal deck bringing in logs. As the machine gathered them, one got stuck behind a stump so the operator pulled hard on the cable to loosen it. As I stood watching, I saw dust popping and heard the clear voice of the Lord. Had I hesitated even for a moment, I would have been killed.

Sometimes, immediate obedience to God's voice is crucial. When the Lord spoke to Noah about building an ark, He gave him 120 years to complete the task. In my situation, I didn't have time to ponder the Lord's request. Whether obedience is required quickly or over time, the key is to obey God.

Thoughts to Ponder

Are you quick to listen to the Lord? There are times when it is crucial to listen and follow with immediate obedience. Even if this is not the case, it is still important to respond to God's nudges as soon as possible. Make it your goal to listen and obey without hesitation.

A Close Call

> So God can point to us in all future ages as examples of the incredible wealth of His grace and kindness toward us as shown in all He has done for us who are united with Christ Jesus. *(Ephesians 2:7)*

I froze. Face to face with a large menacing wolf, I thought, *what do I do now?* Only moments before, I had skipped down the path carefree and looking forward to being home with my parents after playing in the nearby woods. Not expecting this frightening encounter, I stopped abruptly, breathing a sigh of relief when the wolf turned and trotted away.

At seven years old, I didn't understand the significance of this event, but realized later that the grace of God spared me from a vicious attack. Though close calls happen to people often, the Lord gives unmerited favor and often keeps us from harm. And the credit belongs to God who has extended His amazing grace! Although I don't always understand His ways, I know that He bestows grace, even when I don't realize it.

Thoughts to Ponder

Do you ever marvel at the care the God of the universe gives to you? Even when you don't realize it, God watches over you. Be aware of God's grace and thank Him for it.

Just in Time

May God the Father and Christ Jesus our Lord give you grace and mercy and peace. *(1 Timothy 1:26)*

Sitting in the chair, Dave felt sweat dripping down his face. His stomach churning, he held back heaving everything he had just eaten. In the cold and dreary room, Dave looked around at the stark gray walls and a thick, tightly shut door. Anxiety gripped Dave's heart; he would have bolted if it were not for the straps holding his arms and legs. The ticking clock broke the eerie silence until he heard a distant phone ringing. The steel door swung open, and with great relief, Dave heard, "The governor called. You've been pardoned."

That's grace! This fictitious story resembles how a real prisoner with a death sentence might feel. I'm certain those four words would produce joy to such a prisoner.

Everyone who knows Jesus as our Savior has been pardoned much like a governor retracting a death sentence. Receiving forgiveness for our sins and asking Jesus into our hearts activates God's great gift of grace. We no longer have to fear a death sentence as we receive eternal life with the Lord!

Thoughts to Ponder

Do you know God's amazing grace? Have you invited Jesus into your heart and received the grace of His forgiveness? You can do it right now! Just ask Jesus to forgive all of your sins and ask Him to come into your heart.

Unconscious in the Road

May the grace of the Lord Jesus be with you.
(1 Corinthians 16:23)

In the summer of 2000, I lived under Tower Mountain outside of Spokane, Washington. I often ran up this mountain for exercise. As I ran, one day, something went dreadfully wrong, and I fainted. Looking around, dizzy and lightheaded, I thought *what can I do?* On one side was a cliff and on the other, a deep gully. Lying down on the road, I passed out.

After regaining consciousness, I looked over to see my faithful dog lying by my side. Slowly getting up, I steadied myself and staggered back down the mountain toward home. I lay in bed for two days before my son-in-law and daughter insisted I go to the doctor.

Immediately the doctor scheduled me for quintuple by-pass surgery because I had suffered a heart attack on the mountain. After the surgery, my lungs collapsed and my son, who was in the room with me at the time, saved my life by quickly calling a nurse. Soon after, I suffered a serious staph infection. Eventually I survived it all.

I came to the conclusion that it had been God's grace

that kept me alive. Though I have had many close calls with death during my lifetime, God has rescued me and each time I understand grace in a greater measure. I do not take God's unmerited and undeserved grace for granted and I thank Him for my years on earth.

Thoughts to Ponder

What has God's amazing grace done for you? Take time to recall His favor in your life. God's grace is with you. Be thankful!

A Difficult Departure

Through Christ you have come to trust in God and you have placed your faith and hope in God. *(1 Peter: 1:21a)*

Looking behind at my children, my heart sank. Four little sad eyes peered through the living room window, watching as I peddled off on my bicycle. Only days before, their mother had succumbed to her battle with cancer.

Grief-stricken at losing my wife, I left our two youngest of six children with my aunt while I worked. The four older children attended school. I knew my little ones would be well taken care of but was also aware of the adjustment of facing our new reality.

I wasn't prepared for my difficult departure that morning as I left for work.

How can I go off and leave these little ones? I lamented.

Noel, I distinctly heard from the Lord, if you will let Me, you and I will raise these children together.

In the months and years to come, that is exactly what happened. The Lord helped me, providing wisdom and guidance whenever I needed it. Today, all six of my children love Jesus. I put my trust in God and watched as He faithfully cared for my family and me.

Thoughts to Ponder

Can you trust God fully to care for you and those you love? Did you realize that He wants to do just that? God cares about everything you care about and if you ask Him, He will provide all the wisdom you need. He is faithful waiting to guide and direct you.

Cry Out to God

God's way is perfect. All the Lord's promises are true.
He is a shield for all who look to Him for protection.
(Psalm 18:30)

"Jesus, help!" screamed my grandson as his automobile launched into the air, over the cliff and into the river below. Driving to high school from his home in the country, Matthew reached down to pick up a CD and inadvertently turned the wheel.

As the car sank into the water, Matthew managed to get his seat belt off, kick out the broken window, free himself and swim to shore. Stunned but okay, he climbed up the cliff and back onto the road. As he staggered along he looked up in amazement, seeing his own father pulling over. Matthew's dad just happened to be driving by on his way to work.

This series of events, in my estimation, qualifies as a miracle and certainly points to the faithfulness of God in my grandson's life. In his moment of great distress, he looked to Jesus for protection, and received it. I am painfully aware that not all such scenarios end so positively, but for sparing my grandson's life, I praise God.

Thoughts to Ponder

Where do your thoughts and words go under severe stress? Have you ever been in extreme danger when your first response was to cry out to God for help? Try to practice asking God for help in the little things; it will become your immediate reaction in times of peril.

What Do I Wear?

The Lord says, "I will guide you along the best pathway for your life." (Psalm 32:8a)

Is there anything too trivial for which to ask the Lord? Not according to my friend, Merv. He even asks God what to wear every morning—and gets surprising results.

"Hey, that's my favorite football team!" A man exclaimed as Merv walked up in the football shirt God told him to wear that morning. A conversation began, and Merv had an opportunity to tell the man about Jesus.

I don't know if that man put his trust in God, but I do know he got an earful of who Jesus is because I know my friend Merv's enthusiasm about sharing Christ. People's salvation is important to God, and in this case, Merv's clothing mattered. A simple decision put in God's hands can lead to great results for His kingdom. Nothing is too small to inquire of the Lord, even about what to wear.

Thoughts to Ponder

Do you know you can ask the Lord about little issues as well as big ones? He wants to be a part of *all* your decisions. Even the little things that seemingly make no difference can bring a great reward.

Animals on Board

By faith Noah built a large boat to save his family from the flood. *(Hebrews 11:7)*

How on earth did Noah get all those animals on that boat? I asked myself this question with great frustration. Pulling, pushing, prodding and coaxing brought sweat on my brow as I finally got my horses in a trailer to transport them to a new location. Every fall the struggle resumed, causing me to question the wisdom of owning horses even though I knew the pleasure they brought my family.

I wondered if Noah ever questioned God's wisdom while Noah spent 120 years building the ark, yet it had never rained and no water was in sight. He also had the task of making sure a pair of every animal on earth entered the ark. I am aware that comparing my experience with a couple of stubborn horses to Noah's task is like comparing apples to oranges.

When God asks someone to do something, no matter how impossible it may seem, He will provide all that is needed to accomplish the task. Noah's undoubting faith in God enabled him to accomplish one of the greatest feats of all time.

Thoughts to Ponder

How is your faith quotient? He asked Noah to do an incredible task—and with the Lord, Noah successfully completed it. Are you certain that God will help you with whatever He asks you to do? Be assured He will!

Loved and Cherished

> God saved you by His grace when you believed and you can't take credit for this, it is a gift from God. *(Ephesians 2:8)*

"It's a boy!" exclaimed the doctor. One spring day in 1928, my parents were delighted I arrived on the scene. They loved, cherished and provided everything I needed for a happy, comfortable existence. They kept me safe, and lavished me with love.

I did nothing to earn such caring, nurturing parents. Because they were a gift to me, I could never take credit for the solid foundation on which my life was built. By God's grace, I was born into this family.

The nature of grace is unearned and given freely. When we are born into God's family, we are given this gift. In the same way my parents loved and cared for me without me doing anything to warrant their favor, God freely lavishes His favor when we have done nothing to earn it.

Thoughts to Ponder

Are you living your Christian life with the keen

awareness of the favor God bestowed upon you? Just as loving parents caring for their child, your Father in heaven lovingly and freely provides His grace for you.

Lost It All

Teach those who are rich in the world not to be proud and not to trust in their money which is so unreliable.
(1 Timothy 6:7)

Wiped out in one day—my bank account depleted and my business gone. As a young man with a family, I had pursued my career as a pharmacist, owned a pharmacy and steadily built up my savings account. Thinking I was providing future security, I began to depend heavily on what I quickly discovered was an illusion.

My faith in money proved to be a poor substitute for the object of real faith—Jesus alone. Though there is nothing wrong with wealth or saving money for future needs, it cannot be the source of your security.

I made it through those hard times by steadily rebuilding my cash flow and restoring my business but those things no longer had the significance and pre-eminence in my life. God carried me through those days by guiding me how to spend and save. I learned the great lesson of dependence on Him for my provision; not on my ability alone, and I took my trust off my bank account and put it on God where it belonged.

Thoughts to Ponder

Take an inventory of your resources. Your savings account, stocks, bonds, real estate or whatever you own may bring you security—or do they? Can you say with assurance that your trust is in God and not what you possess? He is your true safety net!

Go Home!

> And we will receive from Him whatever we ask because we obey Him and do the things He asks.
> (1 John 3:22)

The words *Go home* came distinctly in Linda's mind. Three times she heard those words echo. One of my discipleship class students recalled a conversation with the Lord that resulted in making an important choice.

But God, she protested, *if I go to the store, I can get the pictures I want. What do you think?*

Go home, she heard in her heart again. As she drove down the road, she had a decision to make: turn towards home or go straight, leading to the store. Once again she inquired of the Lord and wasn't surprised to hear, *Go home.* So she drove home.

With enthusiasm, Linda recounted what happened next. Soon after walking in the door, the phone rang. "I need to get to the emergency ward right away," her friend Carol pleaded. "Can you take me?"

Instantly, Linda agreed, knowing the Lord had sent her home for this reason.

"Had I not obeyed," Linda stated, "I would have missed helping my friend." Later, Linda learned that

Carol had called someone else for help but they were not home. When Carol asked the Lord who to call, she heard, *Call Linda.*

Carol obeyed God and called Linda. Linda obeyed God and received a blessing of helping her friend. The joy of knowing that she heard and responded to God built Linda's faith.

Thoughts to Ponder

Seeking God in every decision can be a learned skill that draws you closer to the will of God. Did you ever think of asking the Lord which way to turn as you're driving down the road? You never know when a small decision may make a big difference.

Carry the Load

Now I will take the load from your shoulders; I will free your hands from their heavy tasks. (Psalm 81:6)

He tripped, pulled himself slowly to his feet, and then soon fell again. "Daddy, help me!" he cried. At age five, my son had done remarkably well hiking up the mountain trail, but it became evident he could not continue.

Reaching down, I took off his backpack and as his load lightened, he scampered along beside me. Soon after, a second child beckoned me to take her backpack, as well. We continued to the campsite and settled in for the night.

Camping and hiking occupied much of our family's summer activities. Because my six children and I had to carry provisions for our journey, each child had an assignment of something to carry to the campground. From the start, I knew full well I would end up with my younger children's backpacks, but I didn't mind because they were my children. So it is with the Lord. If we give Him our burdens, He will take them. He doesn't mind because we are His children.

Thoughts to Ponder

Are you carrying something that is weighting you down? Hand it over to God, He wants to carry your burdens. Your journey through life will go much easier if you trust the Lord allowing Him to carry that which is difficult for you.

He's Saved!

> Faith is the confidence that what we hope for will actually happen; it gives us assurance about things we cannot see. *(Hebrews 11:1)*

Big smiles broke out on the three sisters' faces; their sighs of relief were a long time in coming. Glancing at each other with grins, they knew that the extended time of persevering for their father had paid off. That Sunday morning, a week after his wife's death, he said yes to Jesus and became a Christian. His wife and three daughters had labored in prayer many years for this moment.

Bill, a professor at a nearby university, and his family were my friends. Although a good man, he never took much stock in his wife and children's faith in God. At times, I came along side of them, encouraging continued prayers on his behalf.

Bill's wife died never seeing the results of her prayers. The results did come, however, and Bill became a changed man. His family's faith remained strong for him in spite of seeing no evidence. Fortunately, his daughters witnessed his conversion.

Thoughts to Ponder

Have you given up on someone for whom you have been praying? Don't! Even if you haven't seen the results, keep believing and praying because God is at work. Be assured your prayers and faith make a difference.

Niagara Falls Excursion

You see, his faith and his actions work together. His actions made his faith complete. *(James 2:22)*

Here they were, backed into a corner; stunned at what had been asked of them. Moments before, they had witnessed a colossal, daring act of bravery. Some may have considered it reckless and foolish, but not this crowd who were mightily impressed with what they had just seen.

At Niagara Falls, tons of water cascade over the cliff to the rocks below, creating a breathtaking view. On this particular day in the 1800s the spectacle was even more amazing. A wire had been stretched across the falls and walking on it was a man known as Charles Blondin. He pushed a wheelbarrow. The crowds cheered loudly as he maneuvered himself and the wheelbarrow across the falls.

In a moment of great enthusiasm, the crowd yelled, "Do it again! Do it again!"

They stood in shock at Blondin's reply.

"I'll do it again if one of you gets in the wheelbarrow," he shouted to them.

Sheepishly, the crowd backed away. None of them had any intentions of crossing Niagara Falls in a wheelbarrow.

The Bible tells us that faith is complete when it is followed by action. That faith however, must be in someone far more spectacular than Charles Blondin: Jesus Christ.

Thoughts to Ponder

How big is your faith? More importantly, who is your faith in? Is it in a great God who can carry you over the waterfalls of life? Taking large risks for God can only happen successfully when you have faith in a mighty God who you know can take care of you in any situation.

Spotting a Bear

> May the grace of the Lord Jesus be with God's holy people. *(Revelations 22:21)*

I watched unable to do anything else. My friends and I were camping for the weekend, sleeping on the ground with no tents. I awoke early that morning and quietly slipped away to the river to catch fish for breakfast.

When I returned, I looked up to see a large black bear. Wondering what to do next, I watched as the bear walked across our camping area in-between my slumbering friends without stopping for a moment. My companions slept through it all.

In that early morning dawn, I witnessed the Lord keeping my buddies safe. Completely unaware of the potential danger, they knew nothing about our visitor until I told them when they awoke. God's grace accompanies His people, protecting and bringing them to safety.

Thoughts to Ponder

Do you ever wonder how often God's grace flows freely to you? His awesome protection is present in your circumstances as well. Life is menacing but cannot compare with the way in which God takes care of you.

Go Back to Sleep

Don't worry about anything; instead, pray about everything. Tell God what you need and thank Him for all He has done. *(Philippians 4:6)*

The scream woke me from a sound sleep. *Does someone need help?* The obvious thought startled my half-awake mind. Sitting up in my sleeping bag, I glanced around. Thick tree cover hid the moon and stars from view, making the night pitch black. I couldn't even see my hand when I put it up to my face.

It took a minute to realize that the scream came from a nearby cougar. Sleeping in the open without a tent made me more vulnerable to wildlife in the area so I shot up a prayer, asking God what to do.

Don't worry, came His response, *Go back to sleep.* So I did! Some people have asked me how I could go back to sleep under those circumstances. Going to sleep while a cougar loomed nearby can only be accomplished with complete trust in God. His peace surrounded me as I took seriously His instructions not to worry. When I prayed, He gave me an answer, and I had confidence that He would take care of me.

Thoughts to Ponder

Think of a time when you faced a frightening situation. Did you cry out to God for help? Were you able to maintain peace? You can face anything with the Lord at your side. Even fall asleep with the prospect of a dangerous animal nearby!

Bad Timing

When you are tempted, God will give you a way of escape. *(1 Corinthians 10:13)*

"What was that?" I yelled, whirling around after hearing a loud thud behind me. My dog and I walked leisurely along in the woods when a brown bear dropped out of a tree. Thinking quickly, I made myself look large and menacing, and it worked! What comfort to see the bear run away.

Just as I breathed a sigh of relief, my little dog took off barking loudly in pursuit of the bear. I watched in horror as the bear turned to chase my dog who skirted back and hid behind my legs. *Now what?* I thought. I resumed my menacing stance and fortunately the bear took off again. This time, I grabbed my dog.

That day, I received the favor of God who gave me a way of escape when I needed it. My little dog ran behind me for protection, but God protected us both.

Thoughts to Ponder

Do you recall incidents that left you wondering how you made it out safely? Those aren't coincidences; it is the grace of God making a way of escape for you. Stay calm in times of peril, ask God for guidance and remember that He is *always* with you.

The Entrance Requirement

Let the children come to me. Don't stop them. For the Kingdom of God belongs to those who are like children. *(Mark 10:14b)*

A little boy stood in front of the orphanage door. He knocked, waited and then knocked again. The procurator opened the door and looked down.

"Can I come in?" pleaded the little boy.

"What recommendation do you have for admission?" the man asked.

Taking off his torn, ragged coat and handing it to the man, the boy responded, "I thought this would be recommendation enough." Immediately the procurator reached down and scooped up the little boy.

This story, written by Russell McKinney in his blog, *How to Get Saved,* replicates what Jesus does for us. When we come to Jesus with our sins, pain and grief, He reaches down and scoops us up in His arms. Jesus needs no recommendation: when we come to Him and ask to be admitted to His kingdom through forgiveness of sins, He welcomes us. The kingdom of God belongs to all who come as little children.

Thoughts to Ponder

Have you realized that in your sin, you are like that little boy with a torn, ragged coat? Jesus accepts you just the way you are. You don't have to be good enough for His love. His grace covers anything you have done. Come as you are with childlike faith, receive His forgiveness and enter into new life with Him.

Help!

He grants the desires of those who fear Him, He hears their cries for help and rescues them. (Psalm 145:19)

Gasping for air, the man went under water. As he surfaced, he looked around for help only to see a group of circling sharks. He knew he was in trouble when the winds began blowing. But not until his boat capsized and plunged him into the cold ominous ocean, did he realize the extent of his perilous circumstances.

"Help me God," he called out. Suddenly the coast guard arrived and threw him a life preserver.

This tale mimics what our God does when we are going under and call out for Him. Wanting to rescue us from difficult circumstances, God hears desperate cries and comes to our aid. Even in the worst times, He can provide a miracle if we trust Him, believe Him and seek Him. He will not always do what we expect; but if we seek Him, our gracious God will *always* be there for us.

Thoughts to Ponder

When circumstances of life make you feel like you're going under, is your first response, "Help me, God?" Let it be; He hears your desperate cries and will respond in His perfect way. He is a God who rescues!

Generosity of a King

And since we know He hears us when we make our requests, we also know that He will give us what we ask for. (1 John 5:15)

Alexander the Great was truly great and he displayed much wisdom. It has been said that when a man asked him for financial help he responded, "Go to my treasurer and ask for whatever you want."

Later, Alexander's treasurer came to him saying, "The man you sent asked for an enormous amount of money."

Back came Alexander's reply, "Give it to him. He treats me like a king and I will give like a king."

This account of Alexander the Great is given in a sermon by Jeffrey Anselmi. Alexander sounds like someone else I know. If we treat our great God in heaven like the King He is and ask according to His will, we can receive far above our expectations.

Thoughts to Ponder

How big are the things for which you ask God? When you pray, do you realize the God of the universe is capable of giving an enormous amount? Don't underestimate what God can do. He is amazing!

Don't Trust Snakes!

> Can a man scoop a flame into his lap and not have his clothes catch on fire? *(Proverbs 6:27)*

"He trusted that snake," moaned a young man's mother. "How could this happen?" Having a pet python for years, the boy often walked around the neighborhood with it draped around his shoulders. One morning, his parents entered his bedroom and found him dead. The pet snake had wrapped itself around the young man's neck and strangled him.

Much like befriending a python, certain sinful practices and habits can put us in harm's way. We may seemingly get away with the sin for years, but eventually it will rise up to strangle us spiritually.

Can a man entertain sin or scoop up a flame, so to speak, and not burn his clothes? Will sin not harm us? Just as fire burns, sin destroys. Continual, unchecked sin eventually leads to destruction.

Thoughts to Ponder

Have you taken an inventory lately? Is there anything that could potentially rise up and harm you? Are your relationships morally honorable? Are you watching or entertaining anything that promotes impurity? Are you compromising or practicing integrity in the workplace? Are you holding grudges? Take an inventory today and be willing to make necessary adjustments.

Two Men—Two Options

> Keep on asking and you will receive what you ask for. Keep on seeking and you will find. Keep on knocking and the door will be opened to you. *(Matthew 7:7)*

Two men—same circumstances—different outcomes. Two normal healthy men needed a knee amputation. The first man, depressed throughout his life, never resolved his loss. The second man, however, rode in the Tour de France with an artificial leg.

Two men endured the same affliction yet experienced different outcomes. One saw the way things *weren't* and gave up. The other man saw the way things *were,* looked for what he could do in his circumstance, and persisted until he succeeded.

The first man remained stuck as a result of his physical affliction; the second man learned how to move forward in life in spite of his physical setback. Entering the disabled athletes section of the Tour de France, he completed the race successfully.

Thoughts to Ponder

How do you respond to affliction? Do you persevere and

seek God's plan or do you sink into depression and give up? Choose to live by the example demonstrated in the second man. Keep asking, keep seeking, and keep knocking. God is there for you!

A Son is Saved

> And the Holy Spirit helps us in our weakness. For example, we don't know what God wants us to pray but the Holy Spirit prays for us with groaning that cannot be expressed. *(Romans 8:2-27)*

"Please don't take my son!" Craig pleaded to the Lord in prayer. Craig knew his son had been given only a 20% chance to survive his cancer, but continued to pray. "No," he heard the Lord say. He prayed again, and heard the same thing. As he continued to plead on his son's behalf, he was surprised to hear the Lord's response. *No, I don't just want to save your son; I want to save you both.* In that very moment, Craig knew his son's cancer would be healed, and would never return. God did heal Craig's son and Craig began to serve the Lord with all his heart as he grew in his faith and love for Jesus.

Craig did not know how to pray for his son, but God knew that both father and son needed healing. Craig's son received freedom from cancer and is now a Christian. Craig received freedom spiritually to become a whole-hearted follower of God. The Holy Spirit's intercession brought the best answer for both of them.

Thoughts to Ponder

When you pray, do you realize you are not praying alone? The Holy Spirit intercedes for you, bringing your requests to God in just the right way. In our weakness, the Holy Spirit is strong. Isn't that awesome!

It's Not Worth It!

Now all glory to God who is able through the mighty power at work within us to accomplish infinitely more than we ask or think. (Ephesians 3:20)

"$1,900—but it's only worth $800," stammered my daughter-in-law, Cindy. My oldest son Mark and his wife Cindy needed to sell one of their cars to make ends meet with two children in college requiring financial support. Together they settled on an asking price of $800.

One day, an interested buyer arrived. "The Lord told me to buy your car," He said. Happy to hear these words, Cindy proceeded to tell him everything wrong with it. The man smiled and handed her a check for $1,900. Surprised, Cindy protested, informing him that it was not worth that amount. Undaunted, the man informed my daughter-in-law that according to the Lord, the selling price was to be $1,900 and that is what he would pay.

Both of their children have graduated from college and the car is long forgotten, but etched in Mark and Cindy's minds are memories of God's faithfulness and power to accomplish infinitely more than they could have ever imagined.

Thoughts to Ponder

Do you have memories of God's faithfulness, delighting you with more than you asked of Him? Has He surprised you with an unexpected blessing? The scripture says we are to *expect* such things!

Confused Priorities

Their trust should be in God who richly gives us all we need for our enjoyment. *(1 Timothy 6:17b)*

Marriage can be hard. In this case, it almost came unraveled. While I pastored a church in Eugene, Oregon, a couple approached me for counseling. They were a kind couple who loved God and wanted their marriage to survive but found themselves at an impasse and unable to go on without help.

As we talked, I soon discovered the source of their problem which revolved around their finances. The husband, compassionate for destitute people in Mexico, sent a large portion of the family income to a Mexican mission. His monthly donation left little money on which his family could live.

This man had a good heart, but his priorities were confused. With prayer and a new understanding, he re-evaluated his giving plan. He provided the proper amount of his income for his family and he sent a more reasonable amount to the mission in Mexico. He and his wife reconciled and the last I heard, they were happy and doing well.

In his own understanding, this man did what seemed right to him but needed God's wisdom.

Thoughts to Ponder

Do you ever get priorities confused? Priorities can get confused when you think you are doing God's will. If you haven't prayerfully asked and heard from Him, what you are planning to do may not be the Lord's will. Good intentions are just that—good, but maybe not Godly. Make it your goal to follow and discover God's plan by asking and listening to Him.

Got the Job!

May God be merciful and bless us. May His face smile with favor on us. (Psalm 67:1)

"I wish I had your job." Kim, one of my students, offhandedly remarked to her friend. She was shocked to receive a phone call the next day. The university where Kim desired to teach wanted to interview her concerning a job for which she had not applied. After merely expressing a wish for employment similar to her friend's, Kim now had an interview for a position.

The next day, she was shocked once again when the interviewer said, "I've decided to take a chance on you." Though she felt under-qualified, Kim trusted God and accepted the position as a Spanish Instructor. To date, Kim has taught for over nine years in this capacity.

My friend Kim received God's grace quite unexpectedly. His smile and favor deposited the desire in her heart and He brought it to pass.

Thoughts to Ponder

Does it seem unlikely that God could impart His favor on you as He did for Kim? It's His great desire to bless *you.* Can you grasp that God loves you that much? Don't doubt His mercy and ability to shower blessings on His loved ones.

It's Too Crowded

Love prospers when a fault is forgiven.
(Proverbs 17:9a)

"Sorry, you can't come in," the woman behind the counter said. "It's too crowded." In the mid 1800's, a little girl named Hattie May walked away sadly because she couldn't attend Sunday school. A few months later, this sweet child died. Under her pillow lay 57 cents and a note asking the nearby church to use the money to build a bigger Sunday school for children.

Today, that church, Temple Baptist in Philadelphia, holds thousands of people. God took this little girl's forgiveness and used it to ignite the congregation and others in the community to donate money. According to a sermon given by Rev. Conwell, a much larger facility replaced the original church and children no longer are turned away. Several other facilities were also built because of this little girl's humble request.

Fifty-seven cents wasn't much, but behind the tiny offering was a little girl with a heart to pardon. God multiplied those few pennies to create much.

Thoughts to Ponder

Have you ever considered being the solution when you've been offended or encountered a wrong? Significant changes have occurred in our society when someone chooses to work toward a solution instead of walking away mad. The next time you encounter a wrong, ask the Lord if you can be part of making it right.

Mother-in-law Jokes

Instead, be kind to each other, tender-hearted, forgiving one another, just as God through Christ has forgiven you. (Ephesians 4:32)

Have you ever heard a mother-in-law joke that made you cringe? I have. Those jokes don't strike me as funny because my mother-in-law was amazing and taught me much about relationships.

My mother-in-law married a good man but in his later years, he developed a sharp and unrelenting tongue. Targeting his harsh words at his wife, he spewed forth negativity, yet she would go on as if nothing happened. Without exception, she responded with genuine love and concern for her unruly husband whenever he spoke unfairly to her.

By watching her example, I learned to clothe myself with Crisco™ and let offenses slide right off. If God can forgive us repeatedly, we too can forgive each other just as He did.

Thoughts to Ponder

Can you forgive even if it is needed repeatedly? In those

times remember how often God has forgiven you—perhaps repeatedly for the same offense. Then forgive *just as* He did!

See You in Heaven

But you dear friends must build each other up in your most holy faith, pray in the power of the Holy Spirit and await the mercy of the Lord Jesus Christ who will bring you eternal life. (Jude 20:21a)

"Grandpa, I'll be okay," Kim calmly spoke, looking into my eyes, "I'll see you in heaven." My beautiful nine-year-old granddaughter would soon go to be with the Lord. Her faith so complete, she showed no fearfulness of leaving this life to be with Jesus.

Fighting back tears, I remember that I had recently prayed for a woman who had received the same diagnosis as my granddaughter. That woman recovered completely from the brain tumor. Many prayers went up, yet Kim did not recover in spite of the prayers on her behalf.

I watched as Kim wrote her own eulogy and prepared for the end of her life on earth. Though we were anxious while watching her health fail, she maintained complete peace. A child well-loved, a life short-lived but full of faith was about to depart from our family. Kim's simple, matter of fact faith helped to sustain us through the ordeal. Knowing that we serve a mighty God, we moved forward, trusting Him and holding onto the realization that we would be reunited in heaven.

Thoughts to Ponder

Have you ever questioned God's goodness after losing a loved one? If you have prayed and believed God, the pain and loss can be especially insurmountable. Although you lack answers to your questions, you can know heaven brings a reunion.

God Provides

For I know the plans I have for you says the Lord. They are plans for good and not disaster, to give you a future and a hope. (Jeremiah 29:11)

"I quit my job," Debi shared with my discipleship class. "A brave decision to make since I didn't have another one waiting for me. I worked for a firm with difficult personalities and I didn't want to continue."

Confident in the Lord's guidance, she submitted her resignation and began applying elsewhere for work. When she was offered a position at a lesser salary, Debi accepted the job and within four months, a promotion resulted in her income at the level of her previous position.

Debi's faith increased as she witnessed the way in which God cared for her. Faced with a decision, she had looked to the Lord for guidance. Putting her trust in Him, she received His plans that brought a future and a hope. Debi took a step of faith by leaving her job without having another position to support her.

Thoughts to Ponder

Are you confident enough of the Lord's guidance when He gives you directions to step out in faith? Taking risks for the Lord increases your trust in Him. You will grow in Christian maturity while you watch God at work on your behalf.

From Atheist to Christian

You will keep in perfect peace all who trust in you. (Isaiah 26:3)

Looking up, Larry marveled at the vastness of the sun, while at the same time, he worried about his son. *If I can do that,* the Lord whispered in his heart, *I can take care of your child.*

As Larry shared his story with our discipleship class, he praised God because now his precious offspring who once declared himself an atheist, was beginning to inquire about Jesus. Progress is slow, but Larry is watching his son come to a new understanding about God.

"God persuaded me to trust Him," Larry said with a smile. By trusting God, Larry experienced perfect peace that only He can provide. If the Lord can place the sun where it belongs, He can place a son's heart where it belongs spiritually. God can do *anything*. If we will choose to believe this truth, we will live in peace.

Thoughts to Ponder

Do you understand this concept? Ponder the immense

universe. If God can bring the universe into being, imagine His ability to bring your loved ones to Himself. If you will bring your worries and concerns to Him and trust Him—He will take care of everything. Imagine that!

Perfect Guidance

> But I am trusting You, O Lord, saying "You are my God." *(Psalm 31:14)*

When I popped the question, I knew she would accept my proposal. And she did! I had complete confidence in God and His plan for me when I asked Marty to be my wife.

Many years later, when Marty had passed away and my children were grown, God led me to leave my ministry in Eugene, Oregon and begin a sojourn in Hawaii where I helped pastor another church. Again, I was confident in God's plan for me.

Six years later, the Lord prepared me with the same confidence to leave Hawaii and continue His plan. Not a minute too soon or a minute too late, I waited for God's instructions and at the perfect time, I arrived in Spokane, Washington where I have been on staff at my son-in-law's church for over 20 years.

Putting my trust in Jesus has helped me navigate through many adventures. I have learned to depend only on God Himself, which has paid off. I look forward to God's plan for each day as it is always a new adventure with the Lord. Daily, I seek His direction.

Thoughts to Ponder

Is God leading your life or are you following your own directions? As you continue your journey in Christ, choose to trust and follow Him. Then one day you can reflect with confidence and say, "Yea, I followed the Lord's plan!"

Lost and Scared

The eyes of the Lord watch over those who do right, his ears are open to their cries for help. (Psalm 34:15)

Have you ever been lost? My three-year old daughter got lost many years ago when my wife and I attended a crowded country fair in Roseburg, Oregon with our five children. A day I won't forget!

Each child's responsibility was to hold the next child's hand, making a row with my wife on one end and me on the other. As we walked along, my three-year-old released her brother's grip and got lost in the crowd. We began searching. Overjoyed at hearing a cry that we recognized, we followed it until we found our little daughter. Scooping her up in our arms, we dried her tears while giving her a huge hug.

God responds like this when we have gone astray. When we plead for help, He responds with open ears to hear our cries. We may feel that we are lost in the crowds of life, but God is watching over us.

Thoughts to Ponder

Again, I ask, have you ever been lost? Maybe you're

physically disoriented and confused about your direction in life, or you don't know how to handle a situation. There exists countless ways of getting lost, however, God knows them all and can find you wherever you are. He listens to your cries for help and comes to rescue you.

Locked Out and No Key

Never stop praying. (1 Thessalonians 5:17)

I was locked out. No key. No cell phone. And it was cold—what a predicament! With no other dwellings nearby and nobody else at home, I began to pray, knowing God had a solution.

I inspected the doors and windows but found them all locked. A thought occurred to me: *Go to the higher window in the bathroom area.* Standing on a bench, I checked the window, delighted to see it was unlatched. Sliding it open, I pried the screen off and squeezed through the small space entering safely back in the warm house.

When my daughter returned, she was surprised because she always kept that window locked. Fervently praying, I had watched as God provided a solution to my dilemma. I'm thankful to know that when I petitioned Him, He heard—and answered. Never stop praying and talking to Him about big things and little things as He cares about them all.

Thoughts to Ponder

When you face a problem, do you seek God's solution or your solution? When God provides answers for you, do you respond and follow Him? Father knows best. He won't leave you out in the cold.

Prison Converts

I ask you again, does God give you the Holy Spirit and work miracles among you because you obey the law? Of course not! It is because you believe the message you heard about Christ. (Galatians 3:5)

John Bowers, an innocent man, was imprisoned for a crime he didn't commit. His business partner was caught defrauding the government; consequently, John was found guilty by association.

Prison didn't stop my friend John—he believed that his new surroundings provided a new group of people to convert. Bringing others to Jesus was his specialty. John was sentenced to a maximum security facility where he was not allowed to leave his cell block, much less to travel to another floor of the prison.

While in this predicament, John led some of the most hardened criminals to the Lord, but eventually, he faced a new challenge. When a dying prisoner on the third floor needed immediate prayer, another prisoner pleaded with John who was on the first floor, to pray with the man before he died.

Aware of the danger, John considered the prospect of ending up in the solitary "hole" if he got caught. He decided to take the risk anyway, prayed, and slipped into the elevator heading to the man's room. The man received Jesus as his Savior, and miraculously, not one guard stopped John who returned safely to his cell. My friend is now out of prison and continues to be used powerfully by God.

Thoughts to Ponder

Can you imagine this scenario? John, an innocent prisoner, took great risks for Jesus. After reading this account, do you feel inspired to risk something for Jesus? Whenever I think about my friend, I marvel at how God uses him. He believes the message of Jesus and passionately passes it on. Consider taking risks for Jesus; you will not be doing what John Bowers does, but God can use you right where you are.

Offer Up Your Praises

> Around midnight Paul and Silas were praying and singing hymns to God and the other prisoners were listening. Suddenly there was a massive earthquake and the prison was shaken to its foundation. All the doors immediately flew open and the chains of every prisoner fell off. *(Acts 16:25-26)*

Transcendental Meditation captured Bruce's allegiance for years. It became his answer to life's questions until he began exploring the claims of Christ. Bruce enjoyed chanting mantras that accompanied his past belief system, so when he became a Christian, he asked Jesus for a mantra. Bruce laughed as he told the discipleship class the mantra that God gave him was *Praise the Lord.*

Although he knew that mantras no longer had importance, giving praise to the Lord at every opportunity increased his faith and strengthened his relationship with Jesus. Paul and Silas knew the great importance of praising. While lifting praises to God in their midnight hour, prison doors opened and chains broke loose.

Thoughts to Ponder

Do you offer praise to God in the midst of your prison experiences of suffering or stress? While you praise God in spite of your circumstances, you never know what doors will open. There is power in praising the name of Jesus.

Angels Visited

> Devote yourself to prayer with an alert mind and thoughtful heart. *(Colossians 4:2)*

"I think it's an angel," one of my cousins said to the other. They had seen a man in the woods who said, "Go immediately back to town, one of your brothers has been killed and you need to comfort the other one."

I had four male cousins from the same family. Two were out logging in the woods one day and believed they encountered an angel. When they rushed back to town, they discovered that one brother had been killed. The death was a monumental loss, but these men were comforted knowing that an angel had intervened.

Devoted to God, my cousins' minds were alert to receive this heavenly messenger. As a result, the family was comforted and marveled at God's grace and goodness in sending help in time of their need. Staying alert to the actions of God can allow you to witness more of His activity.

Thoughts to Ponder

Is your mind set on God? Are you devoted to prayer and

hearing His voice? In this busy, fast-paced world, it is easy to put our minds on other things and miss the miraculous. Stay alert. God is on the move!

Record Breaking Days

Trouble chases sinners, while blessings reward the righteous. (Proverbs 13:21)

I broke records that have never been broken since. I was shocked to receive a call to attend a ceremony inducting me into the Football Hall of Fame at Cottage Grove High School in Oregon. Attending school in the 1940s, I never thought in 2010 I would achieve such an accolade. In my high school years, I learned the value of living life to the fullest. It surprised me however, that people would still remember Noel Campbell because of football.

Receiving such a reward was not something I set out to accomplish. As a teenager, I learned to listen to the Lord's voice and consequently heard Him tell me to try out for the team. I played football for God with all my heart.

It pleases God when we pay attention to Him and do whatever He asks. My goal was to live for Jesus in high school, and in turn, I gained a special award many years later. God blesses those whose lives are surrendered to Him.

Thoughts to Ponder

Is your first desire to please the Lord? Have you surrendered your life to Him? Putting Him first in all you do pays off in this world and the next.

God Runs the Company

I will instruct you and teach you in the way you should go. I will guide you with my eye. (Psalm 32:8)

"I had always been a self-sufficient man," explained Erik in my discipleship class. "While successfully running my company," Erik continued, "I depended solely on my intellect. The day came, however, when that no longer worked. I couldn't do it alone anymore; my cash flow ended and the business began to fail."

He came to the end of himself and turned to God. He now proclaims it's no longer he who runs his company, but the Lord. The difference came when he quit trying and began depending on God for his answers.

Jesus promises to guide, instruct and teach us in the way we should go. Before it was too late, Erik decided to surrender his way to God's way, and now gives all the glory to the Lord for the success of his company.

Thoughts to Ponder

Who is running your affairs—you or God? Let Him be the center of your work life. You can be assured that He will do a better job. How do you make Him the center? Bring Him on board as your divine consultant.

Bad Decision!

So he said to Samuel, "Go and lie down again and if someone calls again, say 'Speak Lord, your servant is listening.'" So Samuel went back to bed. *(1 Samuel 3:9)*

It sold for $400,000 and I junked an identical kind of car! *What was I thinking?* Years ago, someone said to me, "Come look at my automobile." It was a 12 cylinder Lincoln Zephyr. The man wanted 200 dollars so I bought it. It ran smooth. So smooth in fact, that you had to put your ear to the hood to hear it running. I had a marvelous car, but after awhile, it needed repairs.

I began to think, *I don't need this.* Soon after, a friend came along who wanted an engine. I took it out of my Zephyr and gave it to him, and then junked the car. A few years ago, while reading the paper, I saw that the exact kind of automobile sold for $400,000. Regretfully, I perceived what a huge mistake I made in junking the car.

Though I will never have that chance again, I realize that I didn't appreciate what I had and I'm quite sure I had not listened to God by making the decision to get rid of that vehicle. "Speak Lord, your servant is listening" is a lesson learned the hard way.

Thoughts to Ponder

Have you ever made a bad decision and became aware of it later? When you don't consult God first, that can happen. Asking, listening and obeying results in fewer regrets down the road.

Ministry in Africa

> Look straight ahead and fix your eyes on what lies before you. *(Proverbs 4:25)*

My friend, Tammy Shannon, a successful New York businesswoman, gave up her work and left for Africa, leaving all to help young girls be freed from enslavement. When she traveled with her church on a mission trip to Kenya, her life drastically changed. From that experience, the Lord intervened and she is using her talents in a new way. I call that full-throttle living!

Tammy still has her business in New York, but someone else is running it. She is now in the process of building girls homes, ministering to those who have been abused or in need of safety after escaping the sex trade.

Tammy's eyes were on what lay ahead. Now experiencing life-changing results for young women in a faraway country, Tammy is rescuing them from abuse and slavery, and bringing them the life-saving message of Jesus. Investing in this ministry with her whole heart, she is putting her time, money and energy in doing what God asked of her, and is accomplishing fantastic exploits for the Lord.

Thoughts to Ponder

Are you "full-throttle living"? Though you may not be called to Africa, do you see those around you who need help? Ask God to give you His eyes to see what you can accomplish for Him. It may be helping a destitute person by volunteering at a mission, bringing food to a shut in or mentoring a child. Look around; see where there is a need. Who knows, you too may find yourself doing great exploits for the Lord!

Live Prudently

Wisdom is more precious than rubies, nothing you desire can compare with her. (Proverbs 3:15)

Have you heard of the famous philosopher Louis L'Amour? He's not exactly a philosopher, but he *is* my favorite author and has sound judgment. He writes exciting westerns and I have read every one. My favorite quote from him is, "To live a long life is nothing, but to live a long life with wisdom is everything." I wholeheartedly agree and believe that living wisely is about listening to God and doing what He says, even when it's difficult.

Recently, I decided not to attend a men's Bible study. The next morning, however, the Lord told me to attend it, so I did. What a dynamic time with Him and other believers! Not long after that, I got up one morning deciding not to spend time on my treadmill, a morning ritual important to maintaining my health. I again heard God say, *Get on the treadmill* and once more, I obeyed the Lord.

I have concluded that wise living accompanies obedience to God in the seemingly small things of life as well as the big things.

Thoughts to Ponder

Are you living wisely? Be obedient in everyday occurrences, letting God guide you in the little things that you might consider unimportant. You could be okay without doing them, but to God, every choice—even the little ones—matters.

The Manufacturer's Design

You saw me before I was born. Every day of my life was recorded in your book. Every moment was laid out before a single day had passed. (Psalm 139:16)

God is like an automobile manufacturer. Let me explain. The Lord makes us all unique with distinct life assignments, just like vehicles are made for various purposes. Some vehicles are used to haul big loads, some carry people and others to race.

So it is with humans. The Lord's plan for each person differs: some are made to help others, some to do things with speed and accuracy, others to go slow and pray, and others to carry heavy loads or carry out different life assignments. Each person is designed for a personal commission from God.

When we do that which the Lord has created us, we live life well. If we allow God to reveal the purposes for which He created us, and run in our lane, we'll finish the race in victory.

Thoughts to Ponder

Have you discovered God's plan for you? I ask my

discipleship students that question and often see befuddled looks. If you are unsure that you are following God's plan, ask Him to make it clear and the Lord will guide you. Why not live life according to the Manufacturer's plan?

Speaking Love Words

Finally all of you should be of one mind. Sympathize with each other. Love each other as brothers and sisters. Be tender-hearted and keep a humble attitude. *(1 Peter 3:8)*

Ten years ago, a couple came to me for pastoral counseling. Communication between them had broken down, leaving them unhappy and unfulfilled. "He already knows I love him," complained the disgruntled wife. "Why do I have to tell him so?"

In many ways, their marriage appeared secure, but one thing was lacking. This wife wouldn't tell her spouse that she loved him. I gave them an assignment to express the love they shared for each other. On their return visit the following week, however, her husband reported no progress from his wife.

"He knows I love him because of all the things I do for him," she answered, when I questioned her about her lack of response to the assignment. Not realizing that love needs to be expressed verbally, she opened her heart to better understand. After learning the importance of telling her husband she loved him, she became more tender-hearted and spoke affectionate words to him. Their interaction and choice to respond to each other's needs improved, causing their marriage to prosper.

Thoughts to Ponder

Openly expressing your love to others is as important as showing your love through deeds. Do you verbally share your affection for the ones you love? People love to hear they are loved!

Surprised by Change

> For all who are led by the Spirit are children of God. (Romans 8:14)

"Do you want a change for me?" Rocky asked the Lord after getting an e-mail from a friend in Oregon telling him about a job opening. Surprised to hear the Lord's "Yes," he informed our class of his impending move.

Rocky drove a taxi for a living but also authored books on the side. He loved Spokane, had made several friends at church and was making this city his permanent home. God, however, had different plans for him.

Realizing the Lord wanted him to provide care for his 90-year-old father, he returned to his hometown in Oregon and accepted a journalist position at a local newspaper—a job befitting his abilities and talents. Leaving us behind, Rocky went to his new destination. We miss him but realize he is an example of someone being led by the Spirit.

Thoughts to Ponder

If God called you to move, would you be as willing and

obedient as Rocky? Whatever God asks you to do, do it without hesitation. Being led by the Spirit is an exciting adventure and blessings will always result from it.

Kindness Won Out

> Since God chose you to be the holy people he loves, you must clothe yourselves with mercy, kindness, humility, gentleness and patience. *(Colossians 3:12)*

Ken asked himself, *why did I hesitate to help?* He told our discipleship class of a stranded woman he met, while reminding us of my assignment to practice the fruits of the Spirit. Ken chose the fruit of kindness to practice one day, and admitted, "I almost blew it!"

On a cold, rainy afternoon, he pulled up to a gas station and got out to fill his car when a woman approached him asking to borrow jumper cables. She told Ken that her car wouldn't start, she needed gas, and pleaded for help. Getting back in his car, he struggled with a decision because he didn't want to get involved. Eventually Ken decided to help her. Retrieving his jumper cables, he re-charged her battery, filled it with ten dollars of gas, spoke gently to her and then left. Ken completed the assignment, and asked the Lord to forgive him for almost missing his opportunity to help someone.

Thoughts to Ponder

Do you pass up opportunities to show kindness to another? Although chances to demonstrate kindness present themselves often, we frequently miss them or turn our head the other way. God wants us to be merciful and kind and provides us with chances to practice it. Be like Ken and don't blow it!

Beauty Salon Caper

A servant of the Lord must not quarrel, but must be kind to everyone, able to teach and be patient with difficult people. *(2 Timothy 2:24)*

"I am cranky when I drive and don't give grace to people," Annie confessed to the discipleship class. She had an opportunity to change her attitude, however, when she reached her destination and entered a beauty salon.

Annie's hair appointment was at 9:00 a.m. but the hairdresser thought it was at 10:00. A little unnerved, Annie smiled and left the salon, returning an hour later only to have her blouse ruined when the beauty operator spilled solution on her.

"The poor girl was mortified," she reported to us, but Annie was happy to announce that her usual grumpiness turned to compassion toward the flustered employee.

Kindness goes a long way, especially when undeserved. Annie extended patience with a difficult person and her actions brought relief to a woman needing an extra dose of understanding.

Thoughts to Ponder

Can you recall times when you have been inconvenienced? Did you respond with patience and a kind word? Don't begrudge yourself if your response was anything but kind; you will undoubtedly have a later chance to try again.

The Holy Spirit Moved

After He has gathered His own flock, He walks ahead of them and they follow Him because they know His voice. (John 10:4)

"I was asked to give a sermon," Newman Hall recounted, "but a prayer was all that came out of my mouth." As this English pastor stood on a mountain summit in Wales, he was overcome by the Holy Spirit when he saw the crowd.

After he prayed, the men were dismissed. Newman did not learn until later that 40 of them accepted Jesus. He found this information to be astounding since he prayed in English and not one person in the crowd spoke English. In spite of the language barrier, the Holy Spirit moved on the men's hearts and many chose Jesus as their Savior.

The men in this community followed the voice of the Lord, not the words of Newman Hall. The Holy Spirit spoke in the language of God and the men responded. I read this story, in awe of the Lord who used a man in such an extraordinary way. It was not about the preacher or his words; it was about the Holy Spirit moving through him to reach the crowd.

Thoughts to Ponder

Are you available for God to show up in your life? God can do anything He desires and He is not limited by man's ability to accomplish His tasks. Newman Hall simply showed up—God did the rest.

Lucy Looking Out

For the Lord grants wisdom. From His mouth comes knowledge and understanding. (Proverbs 2:6)

"Why does our dog, Lucy, sit looking out the window?" my granddaughter asked.

"Because she can't see through a wall," I said.

Such a simple answer. Why don't we use this kind of simplicity when dealing with difficulties in our lives? Focusing on troubles and circumstances will overwhelm us every time. Stop looking at the wall of insurmountable problems, and look through the window to Jesus.

Ask the Lord to give you understanding; He will tell you how to handle all of your difficulties. It really is that simple. Proverbs says that the Lord grants wisdom. "From His mouth comes knowledge and understanding." Where you look matters, like I told my granddaughter, you can't see through a wall. Look beyond it and see Jesus.

Thoughts to Ponder

Where do you focus in times of trouble? Have you

learned to look away from the problem and ask the One who has the answer? Don't waste your time putting your focus on the wrong thing. Look to Jesus and receive His wisdom.

Storm is Coming

When the storms of life come, the wicked are whirled away but the Godly have a lasting foundation. (Proverbs 10:25)

"I looked at the storm and said casually, 'Go away, my God is bigger than you anyway.'" Bruce, a staff member at the church and attendee at my discipleship class, told an interesting account of a recent storm. He worked outside all day on a big yard project and at 4:30 pm, when a storm blew in, he simply told it to leave—and it did!

A half hour later, heavy clouds reappeared and Bruce said to the Lord, "Lord, You can move this storm, too." But God didn't do it the second time. As a result, Bruce got drenched. He dried off, pleased to realize a neighbor watched him and saw his peace in the middle of the downpour.

The neighbor knew Bruce was a Christian and observed how he conducted himself when hit by the deluge of rain. Bruce, a Godly man, maintained his trust in God and handled his circumstance calmly and wisely.

Thoughts to Ponder

How do you handle storms when they hit? Loss of a job, a bad health diagnosis, children in trouble or a money crunch are some of the storms that may loom on the horizon. In Him, you can weather the storms calmly and be a witness to those around you.

Gypsy Ran

> Today, I have given you the choice between life and death, between blessings and curses. Now I call on heaven and earth to witness the choice you make. Oh that you would choose life that your descendants might live. *(Deuteronomy 30:19)*

A dog named Gypsy had everything she wanted and left it all behind. In a story told by Sheldon Vanauken from the book *A Severe Mercy,* a valuable lesson is taught through the dog's choice.

Gypsy, a beautiful Collie, had a loving master, large acreage on which to run and few obligations. Yes, she had rules—she had to obey her master's commands, but they were not unreasonable. One day, she spotted a rabbit at the same time she heard her master's call. Should she run after it or obey? She chose to chase the rabbit.

This began a series of decisions to reach for freedom and turn from her master's loving care and protection. The day eventually came when the thrill to run took her into a dark forest and she never returned. Gypsy's ability to choose could have ended because she never saw her master again.

Thoughts to Ponder

We have the same choice as Gypsy—follow and obey our Master or chase after the life of worldly thrills (independence, drugs, impure relationships, dishonesty). Our choices matter. The Lord says, "Oh that you would choose life." Are you daily choosing to follow the Master?

Prayer for Marriage

> So I say, let the Holy Spirit guide your lives. Then you won't be doing what your sinful nature craves. *(Galatians 5:16)*

"Will you pray for me?" a woman asked. "I want to get married." I agreed to pray for her. Not long after, the same request came from a man in the same church so I also prayed for him. The two eventually met, fell in love and married.

Each of them asked God for a mate, waited patiently, and God answered their prayers and mine.

When you seek God's wisdom in finding a life partner, listen for His guidance. In doing so, the chances for a successful relationship are much greater. God, in the middle of a marriage, brings wonderful results. I know that first-hand because the Lord directed me to my wife and we enjoyed a loving relationship until she went home to be with the Lord.

Let the Holy Spirit guide your life in all decisions but especially in major choices like finding your spouse.

Thoughts to Ponder

Are your decisions coming from God or from your own desires? His ways are always perfect. If you are looking for a life partner, let Him lead, wait patiently and follow Him. He'll bring a match made in heaven.

Act of Service

But as for me and my family, we will serve the Lord.
(Joshua 24:15)

Our class laughed as Stephanie told the story about her attempt at kindness. Stephanie, wanting to help her sick friend, spent the day preparing a special meal for her. On the way to deliver the food, she drove by a man holding a sign asking for money.

She heard the Lord say, *go back and give him your food.* Turning her car around, she handed the man her friend's dinner. The man responded with delight and Stephanie drove home perplexed and called her friend to explain. "Sorry, I gave your dinner away," Stephanie told her friend. Fortunately, Stephanie's intentions were understood and the meal went where the Lord had intended.

Stephanie set out to bless one person, yet her passion to please the Lord led to blessing another who was far more in need. Change of plans can happen when you listen to the voice of the Lord. Stephanie stayed flexible, even when it didn't seem to make sense. God knew who needed that meal and knew what He was doing.

Thoughts to Ponder

Are you willing to adjust your plans to fit the Lord's plans? He has been known to radically change people's directions. Remain open to serving Him in His way—and have fun!

Learning from Fire

> Jesus replied, you must love the Lord your God with all your heart all your soul and all your mind.
> (Matthew 22:37)

A lot can be learned about God from a fire. In my younger years, I spent time in the woods both working and camping. Fires were built, maintained, put out and sometimes fought.

To make a fire, I added more wood, putting it closer together. To quench a fire, I separated the logs to extinguish it. One time, I almost got burned while fighting a fire because I was watching the top of the trees. The fire moved so fast, I barely got out of the way in time.

I learned that loving God with all my heart, soul and mind is similar to maintaining a fire. To increase my enthusiasm for God, I started by getting stirred up through reading the Bible. I draw closer and burn brighter in my love for God by talking and listening to Him.

When love for God consumes me, my passion for Him spills over on others, causing them to ignite in a love for Him. My love and enthusiasm for God can be quenched when I separate myself from other Christians.

I want the fire of God to burn brightly in me so my life will reach others for Him.

Thoughts to Ponder

How bright is *your* fire burning? Are you drawing close to the Lord by talking and listening to Him speaking to you? Are others catching on fire for God because of your influence? Love the Lord with everything you have and others will become on fire too!

An Amazing Man

> For there is one body and one Spirit, just as you have been called to one glorious hope for the future. *(Ephesians 4:4)*

"He's 94 years-old and still preaching," Regg, my youngest son, enthusiastically informed me. Regg attends church in Southern California where he heard Louis Zamperini, a guest speaker at his church.

Mr. Zamperini ran in the 1936 Olympics, and at one time, he was considered the fastest man in the world. During World War II, while flying a plane, he was shot down and drifted in the ocean for 47 days without food before being rescued.

"This man is on fire for God!" exclaimed my son after hearing his testimony. When people are filled with the fire of God, others are drawn to them. Louis Zamperini commands the respect and awe of those to whom he speaks, and passionately points people to Christ. Close to the end of his life, he continues his mission of telling others about Jesus.

Thoughts to Ponder

If asked to stand in front of a crowd to tell what God has done in your life, would you have much to say? Would you represent Him with passionate zeal, inspiring others to know your Savior better? Each of us has a testimony. The closer we walk with God, the greater hope in Christ we deliver to those needing to hear and receive it.

Trust, Rely On and Cling

Whoever trusts in, relies on and clings to Jesus will be saved. (John 3:16 Amplified Bible)

When I was eight-years old, I sat in a Baptist church looking up at a preacher that appeared 10 feet tall. He exuded strong passion for Jesus and at that moment, I realized I wanted to know who he was talking about. Sitting in the front row next to my folks in the little town of Winlock, Washington, the fire of God lit under me and has never gone out. That evangelist knew how to preach, bringing this little boy to life.

Seven years later, my passion for Jesus continued to grow when I read a verse in the Amplified Bible. "Whoever trusts in, relies on and clings to Jesus will be saved." Those words made living for Jesus more real to me.

Several years after, when I met and married my wife, we had a mission to youth, traveling to nearby towns and leading youth groups. When we settled in Winston, Oregon, the Lord gave us a powerful ministry that lit the fire of God in the youth of that community.

To this day, 50 years later, I haven't lost my passion

for Jesus and have been blessed with even more adventures serving at several churches. I want to be remembered for my passion for Jesus and that I trusted in, relied on and clung to Him all the years of my life.

Thoughts to Ponder

Do you trust in, rely on and cling to Jesus? Think carefully about these three phrases. By putting them into practice, your relationship with the Lord will be strong. Don't let your life go by with a mediocre faith but have the fire of God.

Unfairly Represented

Dear brothers and sisters, when trouble comes your way, consider it an opportunity for great joy. For you know when your faith Is tested your endurance has a chance to grow. (James 1:2)

"When I walked into the room, everyone got quiet," Char reported to the class. "They had all heard her side of the story, but I could never tell mine." Char supervises people at her job in the medical field and when someone makes a mistake, it can cause harm. A woman working under Char continued to make needless mistakes and Char had to reprimand her.

In her defense, the woman shared her side of the story with many other staff members. On the other hand, Char chose to remain professional and keep the issue between herself and management. "It has not been fun," Char bemoans. However, she is aware that from this experience, she has grown in wisdom and faith.

"I had to let go of the desire for people to always think good of me," she states. "Defending myself in this circumstance has not been an option." Through this experience Char has also learned endurance and humility.

Some lessons in life are hard to learn but are beneficial to our spiritual growth. Char's faith was tested but she knows her endurance and faith in God have grown because of it.

Thoughts to Ponder

Quietly withstanding an offense is sometimes required of us. Is that something you can do? Like the reprimanded woman, we want to defend our position. Like Char, with God's help, we can remain quiet and leave the situation in the Lord's hands.

Denounce Jesus!

> When the Lamb broke the fifth seal, I saw under the alter the souls of all who had been martyred for the word of God and for being faithful in their testimony. (Revelation 6:9)

"Denounce Jesus!" her father pleaded. "Darling Margaret, denounce Jesus and live!" She steadfastly refused and stood ready for the consequences that followed. The next morning this young girl was tied to a stake in the ocean at low tide.

Given more chances that day to let go of her belief in Jesus, Margaret cried, "Never will I denounce my faith!" The waves of the sea eventually covered her and she died a martyr's death.

Margaret Wilson's demise had outcomes of its own, however, when many people from the town of Stirling, Scotland put their faith in Jesus in 1685. Today, a monument commemorates her death and honors her act of bravery. Margaret remained faithful in her testimony to the end of her life. This amazing teenage girl loved the Lord with such passion that nothing could shake her unwavering commitment to Christ.

Thoughts to Ponder

You likely will not be tied to the stake for testifying about your faith and sharing what Jesus means to you. You may be ignored, laughed at or ridiculed, however. Are you willing to stand up for Jesus? To friends? Co-workers? Family members?

A Godly Man

> In the same way, let your good deeds shine out for all to see so that everyone will praise your Heavenly Father. *(Matthew 5:16)*

Darwin Fletcher was an ordinary man who never found fame in the world's eyes, but had a great impact on my life. As I sat in his Sunday school class, he taught me how to love and care for others. He never missed a session when the weather turned severely cold or miserably hot and his smile greeted me every time I came in contact with him. If the other kids and I talked to each other and didn't listen, Mr. Fletcher was patient and gently got our attention. He never became distracted and he stuck to the task even when we tried our best to annoy him.

Mr. Fletcher faithfully instructed me in the Word of God. He taught by example as much as he did by the spoken word and his love for Jesus influenced my spiritual growth more than he ever knew. He died, but I look forward to seeing him again in heaven and telling him what he meant to me. This wonderful man's deeds shone brightly for all to see and largely because of him, I will praise the Lord for all eternity.

Thoughts to Ponder

Who do you impact for the Lord? When someone speaks your name, do they associate you with Jesus? When you get to heaven, will someone greet you saying, "I am here because of your influence?" Look for ways to show Christ's love to others every day with your children, your extended family or by volunteering your time in places where you can make an eternal difference.

A Child's Faith

Now may the Lord of peace Himself give you His peace at all times and in every situation, The Lord be with you all. (2 Thessalonians 3:16)

"I'm so nervous, I can't think straight," a woman whimpered as she talked to her friend on the phone. "My husband's job is in jeopardy and he may get laid off today."

Her friend, hearing fear in the woman's voice and also hearing a little girl playing in the background, inquired, "Is your little girl as nervous as you are?"

"No," responded the woman incredulously, "She trusts me to take care of her."

"Oh," said her friend. "Then why don't you put your trust in God to take care of you?"

How easy it is for us to be fearful and at the same time, expect our children to trust us to care for them. Are we not our Father's children? He is more capable of safeguarding us than we are capable of safeguarding our children. When we put our faith in Him, we can live in peace.

Thoughts to Ponder

When you face uncertainties, can you trust your heavenly Father as much as your children trust you? When you are nervous about your situation, put your focus on your Dad in heaven and go in peace. Be confident that the Lord is always with you.

A Loving Grandmother

God is our refuge and strength, always ready to help in time of trouble. (Psalm 46:1)

Ashley is a beautiful woman who loves the Lord and can't speak about Jesus without crying. It hasn't always been so. As she shared her story with the class, I sat amazed hearing what God has done for her.

At age sixteen, Ashley was confused, depressed and contemplated suicide. An uninvolved father and detached mother left her hopeless and questioning her reason for living. Only the love of a grandmother kept her from ending her life, and gently guided Ashley to Jesus, who gave her strength and a new purpose for living.

God provided a refuge for Ashley in the form of a nurturing grandmother who led her to Jesus. Ashley developed a relationship with the Lord that sustained her and helped her move forward when she could not do so on her own.

Thoughts to Ponder

Have you been that special someone helping a hurting

person to find God? He is there in times of trouble for you and for those you love. You can share the love of Jesus and change a person's life—now and for eternity.

A Prayer for a Neighbor

> I also pray that you will understand the incredible greatness of God's power for us who believe in Him.
> *(Ephesians 1:19)*

"May I pray for you?" Jerry, an aging gentleman and discipleship student, asked his neighbor after several break-ins occurred at his neighbor's home. The neighbors, people of a different faith, agreed reluctantly. Jerry prayed for angels to surround their property and keep it safe. "No more break-ins occurred," he reported.

He had searched for opportunities to talk about Jesus to his next door friends, but there seemed to be little interest. When the right opportunity arrived, Jerry saw the perfect time to intervene and show how Jesus could make a difference.

God's power, manifested through Jerry's prayer, brought his unbelieving friends closer to understanding the one true God. Jerry continues to believe and pray for their salvation.

Thoughts to Ponder

Have you had opportunities like Jerry did to pray for his neighbors? Many people have a wrong understanding of Jesus and because they profess another faith, we may shy away from speaking into their lives when the opportunity arises. Ask God for opportunities to bring His truth to those who need to hear it.

Landing My Plane

> The Lord is my light and my salvation so why should I be afraid? The Lord is my fortress protecting me from danger so why should I tremble? *(Psalm 27:1)*

Suddenly I couldn't focus! I was completely disoriented and didn't know where I was going—not a good feeling when flying an airplane! I could see the ground and a railroad track below but had no idea where to land safely. I earnestly cried out to the Lord, knowing I could do nothing to help myself.

A question came to my mind. Do you see the coastal range?

"Yes," I replied.

Then fly to it, I heard.

That brought my focus back and suddenly I knew exactly where to fly to get back to the airport. It couldn't have happened without the Lord speaking to me when I called for help. He protected me from danger and proved to be my fortress and protection.

Thoughts to Ponder

What is your first response in time of peril? Do you

panic, curse, yell for others' help or do you lift your voice to the God of the universe? He will give you perfect directions.

No More Glacier Park

> But Samuel replied, "What is more pleasing to the Lord, your burnt offerings and sacrifice or your obedience to His voice? Listen, obedience is better than sacrifice and submission is better than offering the fat of rams." *(1 Samuel 15:22)*

I love traveling to Glacier Park with my son-in-law and other pastors from our church. Yearly, we drive to Montana for the adventure; they drop me off at the beginning of the hiking trail and I pick them up at the end a few days later. While they are hiking, I enjoy relaxing in a resort hotel overlooking the mountains. I especially appreciate sitting on the deck and taking short walks observing deer and other wildlife.

Every fall, I eagerly anticipate getting away to this serene, beautiful setting to rest, read and pray. This year, I heard an unexpected word from the Lord saying: *Your season for going to Glacier is over.*

I cancelled my reservations but confidently trusted Him and obeyed. Over the years, I have learned the importance of submission to His requests. Obedience is better than sacrifice to the Lord. He would rather have our surrender than anything else.

Thoughts to Ponder

How are you at submitting to God? Have your plans ever been discontinued by the Lord? Submission to His will is sometimes not easy, but it is always best.

At the Top

> The Sovereign Lord is my strength. He makes me as surefooted as a deer, able to tread upon the heights. *(Habakkuk 3:19)*

As a logger in the 1940s, I often experienced dangerous circumstances. One day, I climbed a tree about 110 feet high with the goal of cutting off its top, when one of the three cords of the rope that held me was accidentally severed by my axe. Fortunately, the other two cords kept me secure and I continued another 40-feet to the top.

Accuracy was essential in this kind of endeavor. When the top of the tree began to fall, wind could have blown it back and crushed me. If I didn't cut it right, the tree might have split, literally squeezing me in half. After the top of the tree fell to the ground, the force of cutting it off caused the tree to sway back and forth about 60-feet which gave me quite a ride. If I was not securely attached, I could have fallen to the ground.

My sovereign Lord had been my strength when I worked on those trees. He literally kept me surefooted and able to tread on the heights. Climbing to the top of tall trees and cutting off their tops was part of my vocation and I trusted God to keep me safe.

Passersby saw me one day and stopped to take a picture of me at the top of a tree. They later gave me the picture and now I show it to my students. You can barely see me in the picture because I was so high in the tree, but my students grasped an understanding of a time when I needed to rely on Jesus.

Thoughts to Ponder

Do you know that whatever you do, the Lord is your strength and you can trust Him? I knew that was true when I climbed those trees many years ago or I may not have done it. Don't hesitate if the Lord gives you something that appears dangerous. When He is with you, you are safe!

Rescued from a Ditch

> In that day the people will proclaim this is our God. We trusted in Him and He saved us. This is the Lord in whom we trusted. Let us rejoice in the salvation He brings. (Isaiah 25:9)

"My father tripped, fell in a ditch and laid there for four hours," Terry told our discipleship class. This man, an elderly farmer who went to check his crops, couldn't get himself out of the ditch. He laid helpless, though trusting God, until a neighbor came by and rescued him. Terry's dad spent the night in the hospital but fully recovered from the ordeal.

In his time of distress, Terry's dad called out to God and was rescued. Faith in the Lord and His provision can't be over-emphasized. Terry's father could have given up hope, lamenting his helpless condition, but he believed God for help and received it.

Thoughts to Ponder

What is your reaction when all seems lost? Do you bemoan your circumstance or do you trust God for help?

It is so easy to look around and see problems. Instead look, trust and see the salvation God brings.

Contact Lens Caper

The Lord is my strength and my song. He has given me victory. This is my God and I will praise Him, my father's God, and I will exalt Him. (Exodus 15:2)

My son's contacts were lost in the pool. It appeared to be an impossible task, but I believed we would find them. My oldest son Mark loved to swim and often frequented the YMCA to pursue this sport. One day he forgot to take his contacts out, but they came out anyway—and landed at the bottom of the pool.

After the pool closed, we prayed and returned to the YMCA to look for his contacts. The man at the desk laughed at us when we asked if we could conduct a search for our missing items. We, however, didn't underestimate the power of God and began the process of looking.

We indeed found them—both of them—but not without God's help. Prayer and determination led us to two very small transparent objects in a large body of water. God gave us the victory, and we praised Him for it!

Thoughts to Ponder

Would you ever consider looking for a pair of tiny lenses in a YMCA swimming pool? Most people would have given them up for lost. If you know the power of God, you can ask and believe for the victory. When others would laugh at your faith, belief in God brings results!

First Prize Winner

> Obviously, I'm not trying to win the approval of people, but of God. If pleasing people were my goal, I would not be Christ's servant. (*Galatians 1:10*)

The atmosphere felt electric with anticipation. On a six-foot platform a beauty of a car waited for its unveiling. Terry Thatch, a 74-year-old gentleman, pulled off the tarps, and uncovered a pristine 1949 convertible Oldsmobile.

"It took me 19 years to complete the renovation," he said with deep satisfaction.

In his younger days, Terry held the title of champion in national stock car races. Now he pursues his passion of renovating old cars, and wins first prize at every car show he attends. He never drives the Oldsmobile; it has been remodeled to perfection and is only for show.

Terry won't settle for mediocre and states that he does everything "as unto the Lord." Each bolt on the car is lined up like well-trained soldiers. Although they are never seen, he knows God sees, and Terry wants to win God's approval. This car is beautiful and flawless. Terry and his pristine car demonstrate the result of a passion to please the Lord.

Thoughts to Ponder

What is the quality of your unseen work? God notices everything you do and wants you to win His approval, not the approval of man. Like Terry, do all things as unto the Lord. You may receive a heavenly standing ovation!

First Time Ever Said

Three things will last forever, faith, hope and love and the greatest of these is love. (1 Corinthians 13:13)

"I'm touched by your husband's response," the doctor told Colleen. "No one has ever said that before."

Colleen's husband's dementia is advancing. She took him to the doctor for testing to determine how far it had progressed. Both Colleen and the doctor were surprised by one of Gary's responses to the doctor's questions.

"Look around the room Gary," instructed the doctor, "tell me what you see illuminating."

Gary looked around, glanced up at the lights, then to a plaque on the wall reading "Faith, Hope and Love." Pointing to the plaque, he answered with confidence, "*That* is." The doctor, who was expecting to hear him say, "the light," smiled as he met Colleen's eyes.

Colleen questioned our discipleship class, "What could be more illuminating than a plaque saying 'Faith Hope and Love?'" She continued, "If Gary has nothing else, he has the passion of Jesus living in him!" Though memory loss is slowly progressing, the love of God remains in Gary.

Thoughts to Ponder

Does Gary's passion for Jesus live in you? When all else fails, Gary knows, even in his condition, what is most important. Though we may begin to fade mentally, God may illuminate more brightly through us.

Passing the Test

> If you need wisdom, ask our generous God and He will give it to you. He will not rebuke you for asking. (James 1:5)

"You have to have 92% to pass the class, but you do not," the professor explained to me in a matter of fact tone. "Better drop the class while you can."

"If I get 100% on the next test, will I pass the class?"

"Yes," he responded with a chuckle, "but you won't be able to do it."

My first year of pharmacy school had been difficult, but I knew without a doubt that the Lord called me to this vocation. I had to pass the test so I began praying and studying diligently.

The day of the big exam arrived. After the test, I anxiously awaited the results. The professor looked aghast at me as he handed it back. Delighted, I read 100%! Passing the test with a perfect score, I remained in that class and completed the rest of the courses to become a pharmacist.

To this day, I suspect that the professor thought I cheated, but I knew beyond a doubt that God answered my plea for help. I asked for wisdom and received wisdom knowing I couldn't have done it without Him.

Thoughts to Ponder

Do you ask God for wisdom when you need answers to anything you're unsure of in life? Every day we encounter issues and need help from the Lord. The scripture says, "If you need wisdom ask for it, and our generous God will give it." If you are not asking Him, start today! You will pass the tests of life with flying colors.

Throw Them Away!

> What good is an idol carved by man or a cast image that deceives you? How foolish to trust in your own creation—a god that can't even talk. *(Habakkuk 2:18)*

"I threw them away. Every one of them," Bob, a class member, told us. "All my athletic trophies went into the garbage." The day he realized that his trophies meant far more to him than they should have, he disposed of his keepsakes.

Bob reports that a few weeks later, his sister called and he told her what he had done. She responded, "It's a good thing, because they were just idols." Bob admitted being surprised by her comment, yet he knew in his heart that it was true. God had confirmed it through his sister's remark.

He was aware of how foolish he had been to trust in his sports achievements for his identity. They did not make him into the man he became; that was accomplished by Jesus.

Thoughts to Ponder

Do you cling to idols thinking they make you important?

Your car? Your house? Your diamonds? Trophies and accomplishments don't determine who we are. God and his Word establish our identity. What greater reward is there than to be identified with Jesus?

Singing for Jesus

Do not love this world nor the things it offers you for when you love the world, you do not have the love of the Father in you. (1 John 2:15)

Ernie Cruz refused to sing another secular song, despite his fame as Hawaiian singer. When I arrived in Hawaii 26 years ago, his old songs were still being sung, but not by Mr. Cruz. After becoming a Christian, Ernie left secular music behind and recorded new lyrics that honored the Lord. Although many did not understand Ernie's change of heart, his obedience to Christ outranked the applause of men.

Love of the world no longer consumed him because his faith in Christ took pre-eminence. Leaving the world behind, Ernie used his talents to glorify God. No doubt many vacationers to these islands of paradise were influenced to consider Jesus as a result of this man's passion for the God he served.

Thoughts to Ponder

When you decided to follow Jesus, did you leave the world behind or did you bring it with you? Music, television choices, relationships with the opposite sex and behavior at work are some ways that provide us with a choice to follow God's way or the world's way. As we love God and follow His ways, it becomes easier to leave the world's ways behind.

Two for One Special

Jesus gave His life for our sins just as God our Father planned in order to rescue us from this evil world in which we live. (Galatians 1:4)

"I got a two-for-one special," Tracy reported to our class. Her brother and his ex-wife received salvation through Christ after she prayed only for him.

Tracy, who had become a Christian three years ago, had previously attended services where Christ wasn't proclaimed as Savior. Tracy's new understanding of the truth of Christ drastically changed her life and gave her peace. One thing that made her sad, however, was knowing that her brother did not have a relationship with Jesus.

Tracy prayed daily for him, and when he put his trust in Christ, his ex-wife soon did the same. "That made it two-for-one!" she declares. Jesus' death for the forgiveness of our sins is the cornerstone of Christian faith. Tracy's passion to see her family members come to that understanding led to the salvation of two people who will now spend eternity in heaven with her—and Jesus.

Thoughts to Ponder

Is your passion for family members to come to knowledge of Jesus as fervent as Tracy's? Do you regularly pray for them and seek opportunities to speak about the Jesus you know? Help rescue your loved ones from the evil one and be a vessel God can use to lead them to the knowledge of salvation through Christ.

Train Up a Child

Direct your child unto the right path and when they are older, they will not leave it. (Proverbs 22:6)

"You're responsible to teach your children about Me." Wendy heard the Lord speak to her heart when her babies were born. Wendy, who regularly attends the Tuesday discipleship class, home-schooled her two children. She believed it was the best way to complete the task God gave her. During her years of parenting, she heard Him speak further. "Teach them to read so they can learn about me. Teach them math so they can problem solve. Teach them to write so they can communicate the gospel to others.'

"I looked to God for ways to instruct my offspring," Wendy proclaims, "and He always made clear what I was to do."

Her passion for obeying the Lord led her to understand how to instruct the children God gave her and her husband to raise. They are now adults who love God and have not departed from His ways. Wendy received her assignment from the Lord and took years completing it — with His help.

Thoughts to Ponder

Do you know the assignment God has given you? Are you faithfully fulfilling it? If you don't know your assignment, ask God as Wendy did, then follow His instructions to complete it.

Bowling Ball in a China Closet

> Those who belong to Christ Jesus have nailed the passions and desires of their sinful nature to His cross and crucified them there. Since we are living by the Spirit, let us follow the Spirit's leading in every part of our lives. *(Galatians 5:24-25)*

"You're like a bowling ball in a china closet," a friend told Maureen as she stumbled into the schoolroom, dropping books and spilling coffee on the floor. As Maureen reported this incident to the discipleship group, she spoke of how her fast paced life had caused her continual blunders.

Her friend's words were a wake up that led her to review her busy schedule. Maureen realized how rattled she had become, and that had caused flurries of chaos around her. The time had come for her to slow down.

It took years to restructure her behavior, but after responding to God, she is now more relaxed. No longer driven to get things done, she desires to be led by the Holy Spirit. Although Maureen is still learning new behavior, she breaks far less china these days!

Thoughts to Ponder

Take a look at your daily schedule. Is it chaotic or are you being led by the Spirit of God? Begin the day by asking the Lord for His directions then listen as He guides you. Maureen found it much easier to let God lead her—you will too.

Going in Circles

For we are God's masterpiece. He has created us anew in Christ Jesus, so we can do the good things He planned for us long ago. (Ephesians 2:16)

During my younger years, my friends and I enjoyed hiking in steep country. The woods were thick with underbrush and made it difficult to see a trail, so putting markers on the ground every 200 feet allowed us to find our way back.

On one of our outings, we could not see the markers. "We're going in circles," I told my companions. "I'm going straight to see where it leads." Leaving my friends, and as I hiked, I to encounter thicker brush which made it extremely difficult to continue. Suddenly, I came to a cliff and stopped just in time, narrowly escaping a downward plunge. Regretfully, I realized I'd made my own plans instead of following God's plan.

From this experience, I learned a valuable lesson—one I will never forget. Each morning I ask God for His plans for me. Throughout the day, before I make a decision, I stop to inquire what He wants me to do before moving forward. God already knows the plans He created for me long ago. My job is to discover these plans—and walk them out.

Thoughts to Ponder

Do you take time to ask the Lord about His plans for you each day? Falling off one of life's cliffs can happen without God's continual guidance. Ask Him for the plan, and then walk it out!

Holding Dad's Hand

For I hold you by your right hand, I the Lord your God and I say to you, don't be afraid. I am here with you. (Isaiah 41:13)

I remember something I experienced at age three. Some claim that people can't remember that far back, but I did, and this special memory points me to God every time I recall it.

We lived on the Washington Peninsula where my dad took me for walks in the woods, up hills and down into valleys. The sweet fragrance of the brightly colored flowers saturated the air as we walked along with Dad holding my hand tightly.

One day when Dad came to a stream, he didn't hesitate one moment but kept right on going. The water was only up to his knees, but came much higher on me. Though my feet went out from under me, Dad kept a firm hold on me as we waded to the other side.

What a journey it was with my father that day! Safely caring for me, I trusted his secure grip as we traversed the water. I had no worries as my Dad held my right hand. This event enabled me to have confident trust in my Lord's hand as He leads me through life—especially through the tough times.

Thoughts to Ponder

Do you know God has your hand? If you know He is holding you, you don't have to be afraid when navigating life's deep waters. Try picturing Jesus holding you by the hand and go forward with whatever comes your way.

Monday's a Comin'!

> So now we can rejoice in our wonderful new relationship with God because our Lord Jesus Christ has made us friends of God. *(Romans 5:11)*

The title of the first sermon I preached, I borrowed from someone else. Tony Compolo gave a sermon entitled, "It's Friday, but Sunday's a Comin'." My sermon, however, had a different slant: "It's Sunday, but Monday's a Comin'," exhorting the congregation to live for Jesus on Monday as intently as they did on Sunday.

Monday through Saturday is as important to God as Sunday, and He wants you to focus on Him seven days a week, not just on the Lord's Day when you attend church. God calls you to obey Him in everything you do; taking Him seriously day by day. Your life is important to God, and He continually seeks your attention.

Thoughts to Ponder

Is your relationship with God primarily on Sunday when you sit in church or is it an everyday occurrence? Though it's good to have an encounter with Jesus on

Sunday, we are friends of God and He longs for *daily* fellowship with us.

One Huge Dog

> But Jesus overheard them and said to Jairus, don't be afraid, just have faith. *(Mark 5:36)*

"A huge dog was coming after me, Dad," my daughter gasped, "but I turned and yelled, 'In Jesus name, go, and it did!'" Liane reported her encounter to me when she returned home from her daily excursion.

She enjoyed running every morning before going to high school in Eugene, Oregon. When a menacing dog began chasing her, she quickly took action. Liane stopped, whirled around and ordered the dog to leave invoking God's power through the name of Jesus.

When you put your trust in Jesus, you will witness great obstacles being removed just as my daughter did. Liane, now an adult, taught her children the benefits of overcoming fear by turning to God in faith.

Thoughts to Ponder

How do you respond when you're frightened? Do you freeze, run the other way or take action? When you face fear, try turning to God in faith—then watch Him chase away your obstacles.

Out in the Cold

> Then Jesus said, come to me all of you who are weary and carry heavy burdens, and I will give you rest. (Matthew 11:28)

You're out in the snow, freezing, with cold wind blowing on you. As you stand shivering, ice crystals form on your face and hands. You see a house nearby, walk toward it and look inside. You observe blazing flames in a fireplace and a comfortable, overstuffed chair beside it.

As you sense the warmth and peacefulness through the window, you long to be inside. Deciding you have to work at getting in, you look for a key. You frantically search for the key thinking it might be hidden, but all the time, you only needed to try the door, and it would open.

This dilemma is like the difference between freedom and bondage. When you are in bondage, it is similar to being out in the cold struggling to get warm. You cast about, searching for a way to get out of the cold, but it is as simple as opening a door to a cozy room. It's not about our own works or struggles. Freedom is a gift from God; we don't have to earn it. Come to Him when you are weary and He will give you rest. He will help you with your struggles.

Thoughts to Ponder

Do you have areas of enslavement in your life? Are there compulsions you can't get free from like television, food addictions, anger, and unforgiveness toward others? Come to Jesus by entering through the unlocked door into the warmth of his peace and rest, and you will experience freedom.

Bible by My Side

The Lord is my light and my salvation—so why should I be afraid? *(Psalm 27:1)*

Time to take my Valium again had been Robin's thought every time she drove her car. She admitted to our class that fear consumed her when she got behind the wheel.

For several years, Robin prayed, asking the Lord to remind her that He was near her when she traveled. One day before getting into her automobile, she stopped by the mailbox and found a package that contained a Bible she had ordered several days earlier.

The Bible arrived at just the right time! Confidently, she laid the Bible on the seat beside her, after reading Psalm 27:1. "The Lord is my light and my salvation, so why should I be afraid?" Robin experienced a turning point and no longer needed tranquilizers before driving. The truth of God's word brought the comfort and strength needed to travel with peace in her heart.

Thoughts to Ponder

Do you rely on God for strength to face your fears or do you rely on medication, people, food, or other sources?

The reminder in Psalm 27:1 can replace props that you may have relied on for strength. Like Robin, keeping the Word by your side may enable you to take the high road.

She Stopped Singing

> Today, I give you the choice between life and death, between blessings and curses. Now I call on heaven and earth to witness the choice you make. Oh, that you would choose life so that your descendants might live. *(Deuteronomy 30:19)*

In the middle of a concert tour in America, Jenny Lind stopped singing. After she canceled all her engagements across the country, she never sang on stage again.

Jenny Lind lived from 1820 to 1887 and held the title of "The Swedish Nightingale" due to her magnificent voice. She had fame and fortune, but in one day, left it all behind.

Back in Sweden, while sitting by the sea, Jenny received a call from a friend who inquired of her sudden change of heart. "That lifestyle made me think less and less of Jesus," Jenny replied, "and nothing at all of the beautiful place where I am now."

She gave up applause, honor and fortune because she felt she was losing her love relationship with Jesus. She had a choice to make and she chose Jesus.

Thoughts to Ponder

Is your relationship with Jesus suffering? Is the world or your activities pulling you away from Him? Maybe you, like Jenny, need to make some changes to return to the One who longs to be your first love.

Shave Your Beard!

For He has rescued us from the kingdom of darkness and transferred us into the kingdom of His dear Son who purchased our freedom and forgave our sins. (Colossians 1:13-14)

I got creative during the years of my pastoral counseling in grabbing people's attention and affecting change. With one couple, it was a life or death matter.

A fearful wife and her husband, who was hopelessly addicted to gambling, came to my office seeking help. He fell into debt to some wrong people, who threatened to kill his wife if he didn't pay up. He found a way out of his financial obligation, but kept right on gambling. In desperation, his panic-stricken wife convinced him to seek counsel. Sporting a distinguished looking beard, this man looked exemplary.

After I prayed for answers to their problem, God told me to have him agree to either stop gambling or shave off his beard. Surprisingly, it worked! His gambling addiction ended because he was unwilling to shave off his beard. After God freed him from his addiction, he pursued God, making his wife overjoyed and safe!

Thoughts to Ponder

Are you clinging to anything that causes havoc in your life? Any addiction or habit can hinder you from the freedom God desires for you. Ask God to bring you help then become addicted to Jesus.

I'm Lost!

I pray that God, the source of all hope will fill you constantly with joy and peace because you trust in Him. (Romans 15:13)

After stepping off the train, my good friend Pat realized it was the wrong place to disembark. She could not turn back as the train had just sped away. Alone in a foreign country, unable to speak the language and with no idea where she was, Pat's visit to France had begun!

After a moment of panic, she prayed. Looking across the street, she saw the missionary friend who invited her to come for a visit. Amazed, she yelled his name, then they greeted each other warmly.

Pat's friend told her that he had never been to that part of Paris but was on his way to pray for a family in need. He just *happened* to be in the right place at the exact time that Pat exited the train prematurely.

Thoughts to Ponder

How often do you expect the unexpected from Jesus? Stop, look, and listen for His work in your life when you least expect it. God is the source of all hope. As you trust in Him, you may be pleasantly surprised.

A Confused Skunk

Give me happiness oh Lord for I give myself to you.
(Psalm 86:4)

Two grown men chased a skunk in busy Los Angeles traffic! My son Regg called me to tell of his encounter with the little creature while he and his daughter were leaving a soccer game.

As they walked to their car, Regg witnessed a man running in the street dodging traffic. Curious, he investigated and saw the man trying to prevent a skunk's demise by directing it toward the sidewalk away from oncoming cars. Regg joined the effort because he did not want the animal to get run over. In the rescue process, Regg noticed that the confused skunk was darting in circles due to a paper cup stuck on its head. Planning to pull the paper cup off his head, my son maneuvered close enough to reach down and grab it.

The skunk looked at him a moment, then turned and walked into the bushes. Happy to have saved the skunk and even happier still he wasn't sprayed, he continued on his way with his daughter. It did indeed turn out to be an interesting and happy outcome for my son and granddaughter—a unique encounter they will long retell to others with joy and laughter.

Thoughts to Ponder

Do you realize that God likes to have fun? I believe He probably laughed from His throne in heaven at my son's experience. Make a point of enjoying God's sense of humor.

Don't Go Hunting

You are my friends if you do what I command.
(John 15:14)

"I got up at 3:00 a.m. to go hunting but stopped and prayed, asking God if He wanted me to go," Craig told our class. "I didn't have a clear answer so I proceeded with my plans but again asked, 'Lord, do you want me to stay home?' This time I heard, 'Yes.' I didn't know why He didn't want me to go hunting, but I took off my clothes and went back to bed."

Craig, the avid fisherman of our class, also loves to hunt. He told us this incident and explained further about going to a meeting later that day where he gave meaningful encouragement to someone. Realizing that God's purpose for him that day was not hunting, but encouraging, he celebrated the Lord's guidance.

Craig inquired, listened to the Lord, and then obeyed, surrendering his passion to hunt. Though he didn't understand why God wanted him to stay home, he followed God's direction. Doing God's bidding even when it didn't make sense—made sense!

Thoughts to Ponder

Do you ever hesitate when the Lord is telling you to do something? When unsure, do you proceed with your plans or continue to seek God's answer? He wants you to know. Practice asking—and listening—for His answer.

A New Direction

The Lord directs our steps so why try to understand everything along the way? (Proverbs 20:24)

"I couldn't believe it," my friend Annie explained to the class. "I'd been on the staff of a church for five years when I heard the Lord say, *"I'm calling you out of ministry.'"* Passionate about her work, these words were difficult to hear. She asked the Lord to confirm His plan by bringing someone to her who would say, "I love your job so much that if you ever leave, I want it." If that occurred, Annie would be confident the Lord had spoken.

Six weeks later, it happened! As Annie sat in a restaurant, someone approached her and spoke those precise words. Having received God's confirmation, Annie walked away from her ministry knowing without a doubt that God was taking her in a new direction.

Annie states that her health has greatly improved. She has less stress and now works one-on-one with people as a life coach. The Lord directed her, and she followed in spite of not understanding the details or outcome.

Thoughts to Ponder

Are you ready to change plans at the Lord's suggestion? The God of the universe sees more than we can see and knows more than we can ever comprehend. Let Him lead you on whatever path He sees fit because He knows the plan, the details and the outcome.

Look, Grandma!

> And we know God causes everything to work together for good to those who love God and are called according to His purpose for them.
> (Romans 8:28)

"It had been a tragedy for those people when their first grandchild got placed for adoption." Mary relayed the story of her precious adopted son. Although ecstatic to have this little boy in their home, she and her husband realized how painful it must have been for the biological family to relinquish him.

Their adopted son Jack, now eight-years-old, visited his biological grandparents in another state during the summer. While he played in the swimming pool, Jack called out, "Look, Grandma!"

Mary gently nudged the natural grandmother's arm as they sat by the pool. "That's you!" she said to the unprepared woman next to her.

The delight and joy of this reunion remains close to Mary's heart. Since her own parents are deceased, she found deep pleasure in sharing her son with his biological grandparents. Our class benefitted from hearing how God worked everything for good in the lives of these families.

Thoughts to Ponder

Are you convinced that the Lord works everything for good? When you face hardships, face them knowing that God is at work and will bring good out of your every trial. Then share the testimony of the ways God worked it out. Others will benefit, as our class did when we heard Mary's testimony.

Life Threatening Adventure

He calmed the storm to a whisper and stilled the waves. What a blessing was that stillness as He brought them safely to harbor. (Psalm 7:29-30)

What began as an ordinary day in the majestic beauty of Glacier National Park proved to be anything but ordinary! Ward and Cherie shared their life-threatening adventure with the discipleship class the following Sunday.

Exploring St. Mary Lake in their kayaks brought exclamations of joy as they witnessed a large bear ambling along the shore, and watched two beautiful eagles soaring in the sky. The water had been calm, mirroring the mountains as they continued on their relaxing ride while taking pictures.

Looking to the south, they saw dark clouds forming and decided to head for safety. Little did they realize that within 60 seconds, they would encounter a typhoon- like storm. The ferocious 60 MPH winds tossed them mercilessly as they desperately tried to paddle to shore. Ward tried to reach Cherie's kayak, but the blinding waves and water spray temporarily caused him to lose sight of her.

In the meantime, Cherie had been crying out to God to save them. Eventually and miraculously, they made it to safety behind a protruding rocky point. When the waters calmed, they headed for home, cold and soaking wet but happy to be alive. During our discipleship class, Ward praised and thanked God for his praying wife, convinced they are alive today because of her prayers.

Thoughts to Ponder

Do you ever doubt the Lord's power? Even when it appears hopeless, God can intervene and miraculously change the circumstances. Yes, our God is the One who calms the storm.

Hissing Snakes

> You have loved righteousness and hated wickedness, therefore God, your God, has set you above your companions by anointing you with the oil of joy. (Hebrews 1:9)

After leaping through the air, I landed on a log, narrowly escaping a rattlesnake bite. I breathed a deep sigh of relief and thought, *I knew better than to step there.*

Strolling in the woods one day, I tried to avoid a rock in my path. Not thinking, I stepped *over* the rock instead of *on* it, landing my foot directly on a snake. Hearing the ominous hissing, I quickly jumped to a nearby log, narrowly missing the angry snake's response. When I looked back, I noticed I had disturbed not only one snake but a den of rattlesnakes.

What started out as a day filled with joy quickly changed into a frightening experience. Likewise, this is the way of sin; we can go through life not paying attention to the Lord and His ways, and end up stepping into sin more dangerous than a rattlesnakes' den. The Scriptures say to love righteousness and hate wickedness.

Thoughts to Ponder

Are you getting dangerously close to a rattlesnake's den as you stroll along in life? Sin can slither up and bite you if you are not following God's instructions of righteousness. As you read your Bible, you will know where to walk and how to watch your step.

Don't Be Concerned

> I want you to be freed from the concerns of this life.
> (1 Corinthians 7:32)

I was scared! Lying flat on a gurney headed down the hall to the operating room, I had no idea what to expect. The doctor explained he would be opening my chest and doing a five-bypass surgery. That news frightened me since it had been 50 years since I had even *seen* a doctor.

After passing out while running on a steep trail, I lay in bed for two days before my daughter and son-in-law, Laina and Joe, insisted I see the doctor. They saved my life. Nervously riding down the hospital corridor for major surgery, I cried out to God for a scripture to sustain me through the ordeal. Immediately, I heard, *Don't be concerned about anything.* Knowing God had spoken, I relaxed instantly, realizing that everything would be okay. I survived surgery and have held on to that scripture, recalling it often when times of uncertainty come.

Thoughts to Ponder

Do you have a scripture that comes to mind when you

need it? Let God reassure you through a scripture that consoles you, and recall it as needed. The Lord uses His Word to bring us comfort.

Stop Praying for Him

And the Father who knows all hearts knows what the Spirit is saying for the Spirit pleads for us believers in harmony with God's own will. (Romans 8:27)

A terrible accident left my friend, Pastor Love, with life-threatening injuries after a large truck hit him head on. Several men and I began to pray when our church received word of the accident. While sitting in the prayer circle, the Lord said, "Don't pray for him *but* pray for his wife and family." Stunned, I looked up to see another man across from me with a similar expression. God told us the same thing!

We changed directions and prayed earnestly for his wife and children knowing that Pastor Love would soon be in heaven. The Spirit alerted us to God's will and although we wanted Pastor Love to recover, we listened and followed the Lord's direction.

When you pray, ask God how to proceed. He knows the outcome, and you will partner with Him in bringing His will to pass.

Thoughts to Ponder

Do you pray your will or God's will? Practice asking Him how to pray, then listen and pray what you believe you have heard. The Spirit will guide you in prayer and will plead for those you pray for according to the Father's desires.

The Lost Finger

If you are wise and understand God's way, prove it by living an honorable life, doing good works with the humility that comes with wisdom. *(James 3:13)*

I heard a terrible scream. While enjoying a picnic in the backyard, my 10-year-old daughter, Laina, ran to the house to get something, and in the process, she slammed her finger in the door.

As I ran to help, I saw her holding her hand while a finger lay on the ground. Immediately asking God what to do, I reached down, picked up the finger, placed it back on my daughter's hand and had her clutch it tightly as we sped to the doctor's office.

Many years ago, doctors didn't reattach body parts, and our doctor wouldn't have done it without my insistence. I knew I had heard God's instructions, and the doctor finally agreed. Today, 40 years later, you can barely see the scar, and Laina's finger works perfectly. On my own, I wouldn't have known what to do, but God granted me wisdom. As a result, my daughter grew up with a fully functioning hand.

Thoughts to Ponder

When you hear an instruction from the Lord and are resisted, do you stand up for what you know God said or do you back down to the wisdom of men? It takes courage to take a stand in the face of opposition. Stand firm in following God's way, and He will enable you to fully function according to His best intentions.

Spit in the Face

If I could speak all the languages of earth and of angels but didn't love others, I would only be a noisy gong or a clanging cymbal. (1 Corinthians 13:1)

I tried to avoid him, but the drunk man came close to my face, spitting at me while slurring words. Though I started to get angry, the Lord gave me a picture of a mother holding a little baby. Jesus said, "I want you to see this man as I see him." My attitude immediately changed suddenly realizing that God loved him as a mother loves her newborn babe.

In my teen years, we lived above a tavern. It was a common occurrence to see and hear people who drank excessively. That day, my heart softened toward them as I gained a deeper understanding of God's vast and deep love for all humanity.

The Lord calls us to love others no matter who they are or what they have done. In fact, God compares us to a noisy gong or clanging cymbal if we don't love others.

Thoughts to Ponder

What sound does God hear from you? Purpose to

magnify the sweet sound that echoes from those who demonstrate genuine care and concern for others. Remember that only the Lord knows the full story of each person's life, so tune in to God's love for everyone you meet.

Here I Come, God

> Then he said, "Jesus, remember me when you come into your kingdom." And Jesus replied, "I assure you, today you will be with Me in paradise." *(Luke 23:42-43)*

As my neck snapped back, I concluded, "Well Lord, here I come." My sons, Greg and Mark, and I were playing racquetball when I dove to hit the ball. I supposed Mark would move, but when he didn't, my head smashed into his hip.

Though death flashed before me, the next thing I remember wasn't the pearly gates, but me on a stretcher departing from the gym. *Well Lord,* I thought, *I guess I'm not coming now!*

I'm thankful I survived and recovered, but am more thankful that I know—with great assurance—where my destiny lies. I'm ready to go when my days on earth end because heaven awaits me where I will be with Jesus in paradise.

Thoughts to Ponder

Do you have complete assurance of eternity in heaven?

Can you look forward with joy to the end of your days on earth? If not, pray and ask Jesus to forgive your sins and invite Him to make His home in your heart.

Green Apples

Rather you must grow in the grace and knowledge of our Lord and Savior Jesus Christ. (2 Peter 3:18)

People are like apples, I often explain to my discipleship class. My students snicker at the comparison, but it is true. When an apple begins to grow on a tree, it is small, hard, bitter and green. As it matures, it becomes bigger, ripens, and is sweet, juicy, bright red and ready to be consumed.

When we become Christians, we still can carry bitterness, unloving attitudes, hardness of heart and characteristics that don't represent Christ—a green apple. As we grow in the knowledge of our Lord, we mature, soften, give and receive grace and forgiveness, spreading God's love to others—a ripe apple.

I watch this dynamic happen as my students study, learn and practice God's love. Because they understand that people are in various stages of maturity and growth, they have compassion and grace for those whose level of maturity is less than their own. In other words, "green apple people" can be accepted for who they are as we remember that they will grow and ripen! Just as we will!

Thoughts to Ponder

How do you see others? Can you accept and offer grace to those who are less mature in their Christian growth as they ripen? Can you give yourself the same grace?

Parenting God's Way

Give me the wisdom and knowledge to lead them properly for who could possibly govern this great people of yours? (2 Chronicles 1:10)

Raising three boys and three girls alone was challenging, but the Lord met me every time and gave me wisdom. When difficulties arose, I lifted the children up in prayer, and God instructed me how to handle situations. I often marveled at the unique solutions He provided.

When my youngest son, Regg, attended fourth grade, the summer months became a problem. He spent hours in front of the television, filling his mind with information I had no control over since I had to work.

God gave me the idea of going to the basement and bringing up a box of books to set in his room. The Lord also instructed me every night after work to go to his bedroom and sit quietly not saying a word unless Regg talked first. I did this for one to two hours every day, and after a few weeks I came home to hear Regg say, "Hurry up and come to my room, Dad."

By the end of that summer, he had read every book in that box, and his reading level jumped from fourth grade to high school level. And in the process, we developed a close relationship.

God granted me wisdom and knowledge to lead my children properly. Although I did not lead a great and mighty people, I led my children with the help of God.

Thoughts to Ponder

Are you aware that you have direct access to the great help God offers in raising your children? He is the best parenting program there is and you don't have to read books or attend classes to learn! It works.

Mafia Man

> But the voice spoke again, "Do not call something unclean if God made it clean." (Acts 10:15)

He killed seven people as a Mafia hit man. This fellow came to me for prayer longing to know that God had forgiven him. Unable to accept the reality of forgiveness, fear and regret plagued his mind even after three visits to my office hearing the good news of salvation by faith. Fear consumed him so much that he worried something bad would happen to me because I prayed for him.

I often think about this man and continue to pray that he will grasp the depth of God's love. Though I saw him many years ago, to this day, I don't know the outcome of our visits.

The Lord's love and forgiveness is so great that a Mafia hit man is also included in His salvation plan. When we ask Jesus to forgive our sins, He forgives. The Bible says not to call something unclean that is clean. When our sins are forgiven we are clean.

Thoughts to Ponder

Do you struggle with believing that your sins have been

forgiven? Over the years, I have watched Christians hold on to past transgressions, carrying a weight God never intended for them to carry. If this is you, accept what God has done for you. Because of Jesus, you are forgiven, clean and free.

My Mother's Face

My health may fail, and my spirit may grow weak, but God remains the strength of my heart. He is mine forever. (Psalm 73:26)

I can't remember my mother's face because I blocked her out so well, I now have to get out a picture to remember what she looked like. She died while I attended pharmacy school and the blow of her passing hit me so hard that I decided to not think about her.

I didn't grieve my mother's loss, and instead, I intensely continued studying for upcoming tests. I regret that decision. I know that if I had called on God's grace to sustain me, I would have processed her death.

Some of the saddest circumstances can create a platform for God's grace and be used to bring us into a deeper awareness of His love. My spirit grew weak after my mother's death, and my choice to avoid grieving has had lifelong consequences.

Many years later my grandson Jeff died. My daughter's family and I spoke of him often. Telling stories about Jeff, laughing and crying together, we handled the end of his life in a much healthier way. God is our strength at all times, strength to hold on to when trials come.

Thoughts to Ponder

When you have lost a loved one, did you seek God and His strength? Enter in to your suffering, allow yourself to grieve and call on God for help. God will be the strength of your heart—even when it is breaking.

A Book that Saved Me

Oh what joy for those whose disobedience is forgiven whose sins are put out of sight. (Romans 4:7)

"I read *Twenty-Three Questions About Hell* and the book scared it out of me," announced Robin to the class. She conveyed her testimony saying that reading that book brought her to Christ.

Her job at a library required her to ensure every book was in good order. Being an atheist, when she read the title of that book, she scoffed at first, but found herself drawn to it.

Taking it from the shelf, she flipped through some pages and said, "God, I've always looked the other way, but if You are really there, let me know." Interested in reading it, she took the book home and says, "The rest is history!"

This book answered questions about hell, but also convinced Robin that heaven existed and as a result, she became a Christian. Later, she discovered that a co-worker had been praying for her for years. God can use anything to get the attention of a non-believer and He listens to—and answers—the prayers of His people.

Thoughts to Ponder

Are there people in your workplace or other surroundings who don't know Jesus? Like Robin's co-worker, you can pray for them until you see results. Don't give up. You never know what will touch the person's heart that you are praying for making an eternal difference.

Treasure of Life

For God is working in you, giving you the desire and power to do what pleases Him. (Philippians 2:13)

Friends in the class were selling their home before beginning work in France. Though sure of their missionary call, they were unnerved by the preparations for their move.

"Our house sale hinged on our neighbor's cooperation," my friends indicated, "but he refused to sign easement papers required by the lender."

For years they had operated on a gentleman's agreement over a shared driveway with the people next door, but the neighbor balked at a formal document.

The couple and the realtor bathed the situation in prayer. Though they changed the wording on the agreement to cover the man's concerns, no amount of negotiation could make him budge. It seemed certain that the home sale wouldn't go through.

At the realtor's urging, the underwriters re-evaluated the property, and 30 minutes before the final papers were signed they decided the document would no longer be required for the house sale. Only God could have affected this change in policy! Convinced of God's will for them to serve as missionaries, this couple watched as He worked out the details. God's power enabled them to do what pleased Him most.

Thoughts to Ponder

Where has God's will been worked out in your life lately? You can count on His help, even when the details make the situation seem impossible. He is a God who makes the impossible possible!

Three More Years

And since we know He hears us when we make our requests, we also know that He will give what we ask for. (1 John 5:15)

Life had been going well for my wife and me as our family grew to six precious children. We lived on a farm, and I owned my own pharmacy. Everything changed, however, when six months after my youngest child's birth, my wife Marty returned from the doctor's office to inform me that she had colon and liver cancer. The news rang loudly in my ears, awakening me to a new reality.

Treatment for this medical condition was unavailable 50 years ago, so we knew that Marty's days were numbered. Together, we prayed and asked the Lord for three more years to allow me to provide adequate care for our youngest child when Marty was gone.

I quickly sold my pharmacy and sent Marty to look for a home in Eugene, Oregon where a grade school, junior high and high school were within walking distance so the children could get to and from school while I worked. We moved from our farm to the home, and exactly three years later, my beloved wife went to be with the Lord.

Grateful that God let us know in advance of her passing and allowed us three more years together to prepare, I moved forward with my children, saddened but trusting the Lord's goodness. My wife and I asked God for more time, and He granted our request, just as He promised.

Thoughts to Ponder

Do you know that God cares for you and wants to answer your prayers? Despite the uncertainty before us, the assurance of God's care enabled me to trust Him for our future. Can you do the same? Even in life's most difficult times, God hears and God cares.

Love Your Brothers

And He has given us this command, those who love God must also love their Christian brothers and sisters. (1 John 4:21)

"My brother and I, being close in age, enjoyed each other's company immensely," Diane said, "but fought like typical siblings while growing up." Continuing her story with the class, tears came to her eyes as she shared an important encounter with her brother.

Brian and Diane had dissention between them for some time so Diane was reluctant to attend a dinner party where he would be. "I didn't even want to sit at the same table with him," she explained, but that night while praying, Diane opened her Bible to read, "Those who love God must also love their brothers and sisters."

Quickly closing her Bible, she told the Lord, "I'm not going to the dinner and we're not having this conversation!" Again, she opened her Bible, which fell to another scripture in Philemon 17-18. "So if you consider me your partner, welcome him as you would welcome me. If he has wronged you in any way or owes you anything, charge it to my account."

Reading these words changed Diane's attitude and

the next day, with joy in her heart, she contacted Brian to make arrangements to attend the dinner with him. Diane and her brother enjoyed a wonderful time and forgave each other. A short time later, he passed away while mountain climbing. Diane subsequently expressed her gratitude to God for making a way for her to make peace with her brother before he died.

Thoughts to Ponder

An important part of loving is forgiving, and good relationships depend on it. Can you keep short accounts and forgive as needed? You may not get another opportunity.

We are Receivers

> So now we can rejoice in our wonderful new relationship with God because our Lord Jesus Christ has made us friends with God. *(Romans 5:11)*

Radios and people are receivers. A radio is a perfect illustration of the practical way joy functions in us. When turned off, a radio has no power to produce sound. The radio station sends out radio waves producing sound, but the radio can't pick up the sound until it is turned on and ready to receive. In the on position, it can receive sound like music and send it on for people to hear.

This is the same principle with the gift of joy which comes from God alone. We are receivers of God's pleasure, but to receive it, we must be turned on to God and ready to receive. We can't produce joy without God any more than a radio can produce music without the radio station. When we receive this type of happiness, it is then our job to pass it on to others.

Thoughts to Ponder

There is no greater pleasure than being friends with our

Creator. Are you a joyous Christian radiating it wherever you go? As a radio blesses people with music it produces, let your life bless others with the joy of the Lord flowing from you.

The Little Tugboat

It is no longer I that live, but Christ who lives in me.
(Galatians 2:20b)

Tugboats. What lesson could you possibly learn from a tugboat? There was one that had been battered and scarred from many years of collisions and scrapes with other boats. The day came when it went into the harbor and docked as gently as a mother putting her sleeping baby on a blanket. An old seaman in amazement called, "What happened to you?" Back came a voice, "I'm the same tugboat, but I've got a new skipper."

F.B. Meyers, an English pastor, reveals in this story what happens in a person's life when a change of command brings a new skipper—Jesus Christ. In Galatians, Paul describes his old self being crucified with Christ and the new life he experienced as a result.

A life completely surrendered to the will of God is characterized by gentleness, patience, and kindness. Living with genuine affection and concern for others demonstrates God's love. One who is guided by the Lord, spending time praying, reading the Bible, attending church as well as listening and obeying His voice will, like the tug boat with a new skipper, inflict few scrapes and scars on others along the way.

Thoughts to Ponder

How are you doing? Have you bumped into any docks lately or are you living with the direction of your Skipper—Jesus Christ—who gently guides you in your relationships with others? Let Christ fully live in you and experience a smooth ride as you come along side friends, family and those you meet along the way.

I'm the Best!

For God does not show favoritism. (Romans 2:11)

"I know my parents loved me best." Tragically, those words can be spoken by youngsters in many families. A child, singled out as the favored sibling, causes unrealistic expectations for the favored one and painful rejection for the others. As an only child, I never experienced this problem, but delighted in the explanation of one little girl when she was asked which one of the children her mother loved best.

"Mother loves Jim best because he's the oldest.

Mother loves John best because he's the youngest.

But mother loves me best because I'm a girl."

That young lady understood her mother's love. She was well on her way to understanding the kind of love God has for each person on earth. As our creator, He designed us in His perfect way. The Lord's love far exceeds the love parents have for their children. God doesn't show favoritism. Even when you think you do not measure up in the eyes of others, you haven't fallen short in the eyes of God. To Him, you are immeasurably loved and cherished for who you are, not for what you can accomplish, or how you look or any other thing. He thinks you're wonderful just the way you are.

Thoughts to Ponder

Do you know deep in your heart that you are God's favorite? Draw close to Him daily, sit at His feet, and experience the immeasurable love your heavenly Father has for you. Like that little girl, know that you are the best!

Acts of Love

> Dear children, let's not merely say that we love each other; let us show the truth by our actions. *(1 John 3:18)*

"Lists. Every day I had a new list, and I was expected to get everything on it done by nightfall." A weary woman told the story of her life with an alcoholic and demanding husband. She met and married this man in her youth, but soon discovered his need to drink excessively. She stayed with him until his death, and eventually remarried. Her life became fulfilled with a kind and caring man.

One day while cleaning out a closet, she discovered a box full of old letters and the dreaded lists of duties from her first husband. She laughed as she read them, realizing those same tasks she had hated doing for her first husband she was now accomplishing with joy.

When motivated by love, serving others can be rewarding. What was done out of duty for her first husband became acts of love toward her second husband. Being cherished made all the difference. This woman showed the truth of her love by actions. Her second husband did the same by not merely saying he loved her, but by genuinely treating her with kindness.

Thoughts to Ponder

How are you treating your mate? Is it in such a way that he or she wants to joyfully care for you? How could you cherish the one you love? Love is not just a word; it is shown through your actions.

An Answer in the Laundry

> Now, however, it is time to forgive and comfort him. Otherwise he may be overcome by discouragement. So I urge you to reaffirm your love for him. (2 Corinthians 2:7-8)

One day a mother received a letter from her prodigal son.

"I'll be coming by the house. If you forgive me, hang a white sheet on the line and I'll come in."

Driving by his parents' home, the man anxiously scanned the backyard. Was there a sheet on the line? Yes! There was not only one sheet, but several. His prayers had been answered; now he could pull into the driveway and go up to the door.

Seeing a whole line of white sheets, the man knew that he was completely forgiven, and he knew his parents would be overjoyed to see him.

When we choose to forgive, we offer unconditional love to another. The breach has been repaired and love is extended. These parents understood the value of reaffirming their love for their wayward son. It was time to go on with life. Love and forgiveness go together; without forgiveness there is no real love.

Thoughts to Ponder

Is there someone you need to extend that kind of forgiveness? Forgiveness comes in degrees; some people are easier to forgive than others. It needs to happen whatever the circumstances before restoration and genuine love can resume. Press through and forgive, you won't regret it.

Pennies from Father

Trust in the Lord with all your heart, lean not on your own understanding. In all your ways, acknowledge Him and He shall direct your paths. (Proverbs 3:5)

It can be hard to trust God when you can't see what He has promised. I thought about that until I heard the story of two sweet little girls. Together, they counted the pennies in their hands.

The first little girl, Mindy, said, "I have five pennies."

The second girl, Brittany, said, "I have ten pennies."

Very indignantly, Mindy looked into Brittany's hand and said, "No you don't, you have five pennies."

Brittany retorted, "I have ten pennies because my daddy promised he was going to bring me five more pennies when he comes home from work today."

Did Brittany have ten pennies in her hand? No. Did she have trusting faith in her father? Yes. She did not lean on her own understanding but believed what her father told her. Unwavering faith in her trustworthy daddy filled her with assurance that she would soon hold ten pennies. So sure of that fact, she proudly proclaimed it *before* it came to pass.

Thoughts to Ponder

How is your faith? Is it big enough to believe what your Heavenly Father has promised even when the evidence is unseen? Keep trusting until you see the answer. With the faith of Brittany, proclaim it to be so if you are certain God has spoken a promise to you.

Time with God

> For you are all children of God through faith in Jesus Christ. *(Galatians 3:26)*

The pastor's curiosity got the best of him. Every day at the same time in the early evening, Juan entered the church and sat in a pew. Ten minutes later, he quietly got up and walked out.

One day, wanting to get more information, the pastor said, "Juan, I'm so happy you use the church this way. Can you tell me more about what you're doing?"

Juan replied, "This time is very important to me. Every day after work, I come and say, 'Jesus, this is Juan' and Jesus says, 'Juan, this is Jesus.' Then, I sit in silence before Him."

Juan loved his daily time checking in with the Lord. He knew the sweet essence of just being together with his Savior. Daily time with God produces a deeper relationship with Him. Juan, a child of God, took time well-spent with Him.

Thoughts to Ponder

Can you simply come as a child to your Father on a

regular basis? The time when you come doesn't matter. Don't neglect regular visits with God—communion with Him will make your day!

A Strong Foundation

We are justified by faith in Christ. (Romans 5:1)

Have you ever stepped onto a bridge and suddenly questioned if it would get you to the other side without caving in? This question reminds me of a saying I once heard: "I can put a little faith in a strong plank and get across a stream, or I can put great faith in a rotten plank and fall in."

This quote is clearly not about how much faith one possesses but about the target of one's faith. As we step forward on our faith walk through life, we will get to the other side in victory if our strong foundation is in the Lord.

If the target of our faith is in anything other than the Lord, it will ultimately result in our demise. Money, relationships, self-reliance and our own ingenuity can take us so far, but in times of trouble, when we need to "cross over a river" of life, our faith in Christ will bring us safely to the other side.

Thoughts to Ponder

In what are you putting your faith? Assess where you

put your trust and make certain it is in Christ. Anything less than Jesus will eventually be like stepping on a rotten plank.

The Building Code

> Devote yourself to prayer with an alert and a thankful heart. *(Colossians 4:2)*

An intense hurricane hit a small town along the southern shores of the United States, leveling houses and leaving a pile of debris. One lone dwelling stood in the middle of the rubble. Many inquired as to why the man's house continued standing through the storm. The grateful owner of the house stated, "They said my home would withstand the storms if I faithfully followed the building code. So I followed it to the letter."

Building according to code is a wise idea for constructing a home. Likewise, this truth applies to using wisdom as we build our lives following God's code in the Bible and through prayer.

The Bible says, devote yourself to prayer. This means to pray without ceasing, pray for one another, pray at all times, pray without losing heart and pray for those who persecute you. All parts of the prayer code will lead to a firm foundation in your life and will enable you to stand when the storms of life hit.

Thoughts to Ponder

How is your prayer life? Do you pray occasionally, once or twice a day or without ceasing? Do you pray for those who have hurt your feelings, made you angry or cause you harm? Prayer is foundational to the Christian life. Strengthen your foundation by following God's prayer code, it will enable you to stand when all else fails.

Forgiveness When It Counts

Make allowances for each other's faults and forgive anyone who offends you. Remember the Lord forgave you so you must forgive others. (Colossians 3:13)

"How easy is it for you to forgive others?" one man asked another.

"It's no problem at all for me to forgive," the other man replied.

"Would you forgive if you had ten sheep stolen?" asked the first man.

"Yes," the second man answered with confidence.

"What about two cows? Ten horses?"

"Yes, yes," the second man answered again.

"Well, how about two pigs?" asked the first man.

Surprised, the second man responded with a resounding, "No, you know I have two pigs!" Forgiveness does not mean that your offender will not face consequences, but it does require you to release those who have done you harm into God's hands without holding malice in your heart toward them.

Thoughts to Ponder

Is there someone you need to forgive? If there is, choose to forgive. When you do, you're fulfilling God's command and keeping yourself free from the bondage of unforgiveness.

Going to Heaven

> But this is the new covenant I will make with the people of Israel on this day, says the Lord, I will put my instructions deep within them and I will write them on their hearts. *(Jeremiah 31:33)*

"Please don't come visit me," a terminally ill man requested of his friends. An agnostic acquaintance visited him and afterwards, he asked, "Why won't you let your other friends see you, but you allowed me to visit?" The ill man smiled and said, "I will see them in heaven, but I may not see you ever again."

This dying man spoke great wisdom and hopefully encouraged his acquaintance to consider the claims of Christ. God gives us words to speak when we need them, enabling us to handle each situation.

God-given wisdom brings instructions for daily living and helps us have a productive existence. God told the people of Israel long ago that He would write His instructions upon their hearts, and He does the same with us today. His wisdom impacts the people we know, even to our dying day.

Thoughts to Ponder

Do you speak your own words or words of wisdom from God? Let God speak through you. What you say could have an eternal impact on someone's life.

Little Girl Teacher

And because they love Me, my Father will love them. and I will love them and reveal Myself to each of them. (John 14:21b)

"I am the teacher," announced a little twelve-year-old girl. Robert Maffat inquired who taught in the Christian school in a small remote village and was surprised to hear this shy child's response. In fact, when he read a sign indicating there *was* a Christian school in this village, he was amazed.

Robert had come to the back country of Africa as a missionary in the 1800's assuming that the people had never heard of Jesus. Now he talked to a little girl claiming to be teaching that very message. Inquiring further, he learned that this child had been taken to a distant tribe where she heard about the Lord from another missionary.

This youngster had a passion for God and, at a tender age, began spreading the good news to her own tribe when she returned. God revealed Himself to her and He will reveal Himself to anyone. His message can be spread to others by people of any age.

Thoughts to Ponder

Is God's word going forth through you? You don't have to start a school or go to Africa to spread the Word of God. Telling your friends and family how the Lord changed your life is a good start.

Why Aren't You Here?

> But others were tortured, refusing to turn from God in order to be set free. They placed their hope in a better life after the resurrection. Some were jeered at and their backs were cut open with whips. Others were chained in prison. *(Hebrews 11:35b-36)*

"Why are you here in prison?" a chaplain inquired of Brother Yun.

Brother Yun responded, "Why aren't *you* here?" A witness for Christ in China, Mr. Yun was apprehended by Chinese officials, a fate endured by those who openly profess their belief in Jesus.

The question posed to this chaplain must have caused him to ponder his effectiveness as a Christian. Sharing Christ with others in some countries can bring risk of imprisonment, torture and even the possibility of death. However, there are those whose devotion to the Lord does not include taking such risks.

Thoughts to Ponder

Is your witness for Jesus strong enough to put you in prison? In America, that isn't a concern, though you may be asked to boldly share the love of Christ with a neighbor, co-worker or loved one. Are you willing to take a risk for Him?

From Heathens to Christians

So we keep on praying for you, asking our God to enable you to life a live worthy of His call. May He give you the power to accomplish all the good things your faith prompts you to do. (2 Thessalonians 2:11)

"When he came, there were no Christians, when he died, there were no heathens."

The headstone of John Geddie bore those profound words. Geddie, an amazing missionary, worked with the natives of the South Seas who were in tremendous satanic bondage. Geddie never gave up on them.

His entire career centered on bringing the message of Christ to these tribes. When he died among the tribe people he loved, his tombstone clearly indicated the success of his mission.

When the Lord asks you to do something, He equips and enables you to accomplish it. With the Lord, Geddie faithfully fulfilled God's call, and as a result, many are in heaven.

Thoughts to Ponder

What will your tombstone reveal about you? Will heaven

acknowledge your effectiveness for Christ on earth? Though God wants us to enjoy ourselves, living for Christ and accomplishing His tasks can leave a great legacy.

Secret of Contentment

Not that I was ever in need, for I have learned how to be content in whatever I have. (Philippians 2:14)

Do you ever want what you don't have? I did until I heard this saying:

"God gave us spring, but it was summer I really wanted with warm days and time outdoors. Summer came, but it was fall I really wanted with the nice crisp days. I didn't realize how hot it would be in the summer. Fall came, but it was winter I really wanted thinking about the holidays and fun in the snow. Winter came, but it was spring I really wanted...."

How often we take what we have for granted, not appreciating it, and thinking something else would be better. Remember Paul? He was shipwrecked, bitten by a viperous snake, and chained in prison, but in the midst of it all, he declared, "I have learned to be content in whatever I have." Paul learned the secret of contentment in all circumstances, demonstrating the wisdom of accepting our current circumstances as God's plan. If our attitude is correct, with whatever we have or wherever we are, we will be content.

Summer, fall, winter, spring—God makes the changing seasons. God also brings about our circumstances or allows them to take place. Knowing that fact, we can enjoy peace at all times.

Thoughts to Ponder

Are you content with your present circumstances or do you continually look for something to make life better? Is your spouse, work, children, home, finances or circumstances enough to bring you joy? Can you be content even when life brings hardships? Focus less on your circumstances and more on your attitude and appreciate each season in which you live.

The Cave and the Sun

> This is the message we heard from Jesus and now declare to you. God is light and there is no darkness in Him at all. *(1 John 1:5)*

The parable of the cave and the sun is a powerful tale; here's how it goes:

Cave lived underground and spent its life in darkness. One day, the cave heard a call, "Come to the light."

"I don't know what you mean," said the cave.

The sun responded, "Then I will come into the cave."

"Good, come in and see my darkness," answered the cave.

Sun replied, "What's darkness?"

Cave said, "Come and see."

The sun came into the cave saying, "Now show me your darkness." But there was no darkness because the sun had brought the light.

This parable is a perfect example of how the light of God drives out sin and darkness. This light comes when we ask Jesus to become our Savior; it dispels the darkness of sin because God is light and in Him there is no darkness.

Thoughts to Ponder

Do you live in light or darkness? When you pray to receive Jesus as your Savior and ask Him to forgive your sins, the darkness must go because the light has come and dwells within you. Let your light shine!

Minnesota Miracle

> Elijah was as human as we are, and yet when he prayed earnestly that no rain would fall, none fell for three and a half years. *(James 5:17)*

In the state of Minnesota a hundred years ago, the miraculous happened. Things were not going well when for three years; the people of that state endured thousands of locusts destroying their crops and leaving them in financial ruin.

The governor, a godly man, went into action and proclaimed a day of prayer. The whole state shut down while the Minnesotans fervently prayed, but answers did not come the way the people expected. After their prayers, a heat wave came and the locust eggs hatched, dramatically *increasing* the locust population. The people of the state were greatly distressed until the miracle came—a freeze covered the state and all of the insects died!

God knew exactly how to perform the miracle and answer the pleas of the people. Like God stopped the rain when Elijah prayed in the Old Testament, He stopped the locusts from devastating Minnesota when its people prayed. Believing prayer can accomplish great things!

Thoughts to Ponder

Do you pray and believe that God will hear and answer? Sometimes we pray half-heartedly, doubting that our prayer will be answered. Ponder your faith that accompanies your prayer. Does it need to increase?

About The Authors

Noel Campbell was born in 1928 in Aberdeen, Washington to Christian parents. He graduated from high school in Cottage Grove, Oregon and worked in the logging industry before attending college where he received a degree in pharmacy from Oregon State College. Noel married Marty in September 1951 and they had six children, three sons and three daughters. Marty went to be with the Lord 17 years later in 1968.

Noel was a pharmacist for 25 years and a part-time youth pastor to hundreds of teens who met in the family home. He also mentored six men who became pastors. Noel became a full-time pastor in 1973 and has served at churches in Washington, Oregon and Hawaii.

In 2000, he began teaching discipleship classes at Life Center Church in Spokane, Washington. He lives with his daughter and son-in-law, the senior pastor of Life Center, a Foursquare church of 4,000 attendees.

Linda Hanke is a freelance writer and social worker. After receiving her Masters in Social Work Degree in 1980, she has worked with young women, providing support in life decisions and parenting their young children. She directed a maternity home in a Crisis Pregnancy Center for six years and worked for several foster care and adoption agencies, placing children in loving Christian homes.

She lives in Spokane, Washington, has two grown children and four grandchildren.

She has written several articles for Christian magazines, newspapers and *Closer to God, True Stories of Answers to Prayer*, a Guideposts publication.